QUALITY IS PERSONAL

QUALITY IS PERSONAL

A FOUNDATION FOR TOTAL QUALITY MANAGEMENT

Harry V. Roberts

Bernard F. Sergesketter

THE FREE PRESS
A Division of Macmillan, Inc.
NEW YORK

Maxwell Macmillan Canada
TORONTO
Maxwell Macmillan International
NEW YORK   OXFORD   SINGAPORE   SYDNEY

The Free Press
A Division of Macmillan, Inc.
866 Third Avenue, New York, N. Y. 10022

Maxwell Macmillan Canada, Inc.
1200 Eglinton Avenue East
Suite 200
Don Mills, Ontario M3C 3N1

Macmillan, Inc. is part of the Maxwell Communication
Group of Companies.

Printed in the United States of America

printing number

2 3 4 5 6 7 8 9 10

Library of Congress Cataloging–in–Publication Data

Roberts, Harry V.
    Quality is personal: a foundation for total quality management /
Harry V. Roberts, Bernard F. Sergesketter.
        p.   cm.
    Includes index.
    ISBN 0–02–926626–2 (cloth).—ISBN 0–02–926625–4 (pbk.)
    1. Total quality management.   I. Sergesketter, Bernard F.
II. Title.
HD62.15.R63   1993
658.5'62—dc20   93–21723
                                                          CIP

To June, DD, Andy, Celine,
and V-Squared

Harry

To Mary, whose love and
friendship I cherish

Bernie

CONTENTS

FOREWORD

The authors have hit the bullseye! Quality *is* personal.

Since 1988 I probably have interfaced with more American business leaders on the subject of quality than any other general business executive. Most of these executives are raising their corporate sights and systems on quality, and impressively manifesting their dedication to new levels of achievement. All of them acknowledge that "the boss" has to be an involved believer if quality is to be a key culture, practice, and result in their renewing companies.

But no one has bought in more quickly or as practically as Bernie Sergesketter. He tells of that profound initial buy-in and has demonstrated from the initial moment on, the most effective personal role modelship vis-à-vis quality by any senior executive that I know of.

Harry Roberts, a proven influence in the study of quality, has revitalized his advanced teachings on the subject, rallying off Bernie's example.

Together they bring a new dimension to the personal leadership and management of quality that, to the best of my knowledge, has rarely been employed. As they spell it out—as Bernie does it day in, day out, and as Harry exercises it in his key classes—you will be introduced to a simple tool with a profound effect.

The two of them were kind to invite me to inscribe this foreword. I consider it a privilege to acknowledge that their basic idea is the single most powerful concept to leverage the personal leadership of the quality process since the Malcolm Baldrige National Quality Award reawakened America's energies in behalf of satisfying the highest quality expectations by industry.

Robert W. Galvin
Chairman of the Executive Committee
Motorola, Inc.

TIPS FOR THE READER

The concepts of personal quality set forth in this book can be useful to you, and soon. You don't have to read the whole book in order to get started, and the book will be easier and more rewarding to read if you are actually applying the concepts to your own work and life.

A quick reading of Chapters 1 through 2 will convey the general idea, and get you started with an initial personal quality checklist. It is well not to freeze your checklist immediately, but to start recording defects for a few days, permitting yourself to revise standards as necessary. While you are doing this, you can skim Chapter 3 to get ideas about additional standards that might help you.

The rest of the book can be browsed at any time. Detailed reading can be reserved for those topics that most intrigue you. Repeated browsing is likely to be more effective than a single sustained reading. Chapter 4 gives several approaches to personal quality improvement that do not employ checklists. These will be most useful after you are well on the way to using and benefiting from your personal quality checklist; for some readers, they may even be applied before the checklist is made. In any event, it is Chapter 4 that will show how to maintain the momentum of continuous improvement.

Chapter 5 extends ideas of personal quality to organizational quality. The Appendix gives nontechnical ideas of statistical analysis for your defect counts in order to assess whether you are improving, and by how much. The statistical emphasis is on simple graphical techniques and visual interpretation of the graphs.

ACKNOWLEDGMENTS

We were fortunate to have the support of many people in developing the concepts in this book. From the very start, Bob Galvin offered us his encouragement and inspiration, and he shared his knowledge and insights with us. Bob cares very deeply about quality, and we learned much by just observing the way he works. Bob's associates at Motorola, particularly Paul Noakes, Bill Smith, and Keki Bhote helped us and told us we were pursuing something worthwhile.

We thank Tink Campbell for bringing the two of us together. As president of the Chicago Presidents Organization, Tink asked each of us to speak at a Quality Forum for that group in August of 1991, and that is how we met. Tink is devoted to quality and has made Total Quality Management a way of life in his company.

We appreciate the support and participation of many people at AT&T. Bob Allen set the stage for the importance of quality several years ago. He is committed to delighting customers, and he believes deeply that quality happens through people. Phil Scanlan, AT&T's quality vice president, has a wonderful depth of knowledge in quality and was most generous with his advice and counsel. Linda Brand, Mary Rodino, Roberta Coleman, Bill Fuess, and Pat Black are all experts in quality and encouraged the use of the concepts in this book with their associates. There isn't enough room to acknowledge all of the other people in AT&T who were helpful, particularly those in the Central Region of Business Network Sales.

For the first intensive student tryouts of the concepts presented in this book, we are grateful to students in the 62nd group of the Executive Program, Graduate School of Business, University of Chicago, to students in subsequent MBA classes in quality and productivity improvement at Chicago, and to participants in the Chicago Presidents Organization Total Quality Forum in 1991–1992. Attendees at many short courses and talks have provided valuable feedback. Many of these contributions appear directly in the book, although examples of applications are presented anonymously to maintain confidentiality.

We have also drawn on ideas from many people knowledgeable in business and quality management, starting chronologically with Benjamin Franklin; we have presented their names along with their ideas, so that all these contributions are reflected in the index. So many colleagues at the University of Chicago have stimulated our efforts that any short enumeration is bound to be incomplete; however, we must explicitly mention George Bateman, Selwyn Becker, Harry Davis, George Easton, Tim Fuller, Abbie Griffin, Bill Golomski, Robert Kenmore, Bill Kooser, Al Madansky, and Bill Zangwill.

The people at The Free Press were great throughout the project. In particular we thank Bob Wallace, Lisa Cuff, Robert Harrington, Linnea Johnson, and Kay Wahrsager for all that they added along the way.

We received wonderful support from our families during our writing of this book, and that is special to us. They encouraged us and were patient with us, and they enabled us.

To all of you, named and unnamed, who helped us in so many ways, our sincere thanks.

INTRODUCTION

Many of us would like to learn more about quality and also do a better job of meeting our professional and personal goals. That is what this book is about. Its concepts are straightforward, and they have been proven to be very effective.

Today's quality principles have their roots in improving manufacturing processes with a focus on how machines function. We have applied these principles to the way people live and work, taking into account human aspirations and needs for fulfillment. The lesson we learned is that the fundamental principles of quality apply to all work and are just as relevant to services as they are to manufacturing.

There is, however, another key lesson, which is the basis of our beliefs. Quality as practiced by the individual is the foundation on which Total Quality Management is built. Quality is based on the actions of people. Total Quality Management cannot exist without all the people in an organization understanding and practicing the principles of quality at a personal level.

Bob Galvin, a world leader in Total Quality Management, spoke about the personal aspects of quality in an address to the Economic Club of Chicago. He said that quality used to be a corporate way of life; now it has also become a personal one:

> We have operated very substantially under the rubric of quality control. Our institutions, our companies have had quality departments. And the old testament was that quality is a company, a department, and an institutional responsibility.

> The new truth is radically different. Quality is a very personal obligation. If you can't talk about quality in the first person . . . then you have not moved to the level of involvement of quality that is absolutely essential. [This] . . . is the most useful thing I can say. . . . You must be a believer that quality is a very personal responsibility.

This book will show you how to apply the principles of quality to all that you do as an individual. It will show you how to improve your personal performance as well as the performance of your organization or team, and it will show you how to hold the gains.

Harry Roberts
Bernie Sergesketter

QUALITY IS PERSONAL

1

QUALITY, PERSONAL QUALITY, AND PERSONAL QUALITY CHECKLISTS

1. QUALITY AND TOTAL QUALITY MANAGEMENT

Although our primary interest is quality for the individual—in work and in everyday life—we begin with a brief survey of organizational quality, or, as it is frequently called, Total Quality Management (TQM). (Parts of this survey are drawn from the Report of the Working Council on Core Body of Knowledge for the Procter & Gamble Total Quality Forum of 1992.)

The working assumption of TQM is that continual organizational improvements, *small and large*, are not only possible but are necessary for long-term survival. Opportunities for improvement are recognized primarily by continuing reexamination of *all* existing constraints on the way that work is done. This reexamination is focused on all organizational processes, and it is guided by three basic ideas, which have to be sold to all employees:

1. Orient all efforts towards delighting customers and removing waste in (or constraints on) internal processes.
2. Stress team effort at all levels inside and outside the organization, including cooperative efforts with suppliers and customers.
3. Use data and scientific reasoning to guide and evaluate improvement efforts, and to hold the gains from past improvements.

These three ideas, when applied systematically, lead to management practices that are very different from traditional practices. The new practices are so appealing that many people, upon first encountering them, will insist that they have been following them all along.

The ideas of TQM lead to much more than meets the eye on first glance. And they pose a profound psychological challenge: they say that, no matter what we have done in our lives up to now, we must be prepared to find that we can do enormously better. This is gratifying in the sense that improvement is always gratifying. But it also suggests that what we have done in the past is going to look bad in the light of present knowledge. For many of us, that is hard to accept.

The detailed management tactics of TQM go beyond traditional optimization within fixed constraints to shoot at ever-moving improvement targets by relaxing or eliminating constraints. Since there is no end to opportunities to relax or eliminate constraints, improvement is never ending.

Relaxing Constraints

"Relaxing a constraint" is an abstract expression. One of the authors offers a personal example of what it means. In 1968 the author and his teenage son were jogging along a mountain trail in North Carolina when they were confronted by a large eastern timber rattlesnake who was visibly and noisily blocking the trail. They stopped abruptly about ten yards short of the rattler. The father picked up a large dead branch and advanced on the snake, intending to make him move off the trail so that they could continue the run. The son called out in alarm, "Dad, let's just walk around him!"

They took a wide semicircle around the snake and continued on their way. The rattler went on rattling, but the confrontation had been avoided. Here, the constraint was the assumption that the process of jogging demanded that they stay on the trail; the removal of the constraint permitted the run to continue without a potentially disastrous incident.

A Definition of TQM

TQM is a people-focused management system that aims at continual increase of customer satisfaction at continually lower real cost. This is a total system approach (not a separate area or program), and an integral part of high-level strategy; it works horizontally across functions and departments, involves all employees, top to bottom, and extends backward and forward to include the supply chain and the customer chain.

TQM stresses learning and adaptation to continual change as keys to organizational success.

The foundation of TQM is philosophical: the scientific method. It includes systems, methods, and tools. The systems permit change; the philosophy stays the same. TQM is anchored in values that stress the dignity of the individual and the power of community action.

TQM is in one sense a highly democratic system, but it requires dedicated and informed leadership from senior management, leadership that is aware of the obstacles to successful implementation. TQM goes beyond specific improvements, however desirable these may be, to the transformation of organizations and organizational cultures from what they are today to something very different.

What Is In an Acronym?

TQM is only one of many acronyms used to label the management system that we have just described. Some of these acronyms are widely used, especially CQI for Continuous Quality Improvement. Others are specific to given companies or organizations. Three comments are in order:

- ° The substance that underlies the acronym is what matters.
- ° Labeling a given organization's activities by one of these acronyms does not in itself demonstrate that the organization is implementing the management system we are discussing.
- ° All the current acronyms could pass out of use without affecting the usefulness of the management system here described. An organization could implement the concepts without using any acronym at all.

Definition of Quality

This approach to TQM suggests that customer satisfaction—even customer delight—is a useful definition of "quality." Customer satisfaction has many dimensions, of which conformance to specifications* is only one. In addition, in *Building a Chain of Customers* (New York: The Free Press, 1988), Richard Schonberger, distinguishes:

- performance*
- quick (some suggest "timely") response
- quick change expertise
- features*
- reliability*
- durability*
- serviceability*
- aesthetics*
- perceived quality*
- humanity
- value

The eight starred items are taken from a listing by David Garvin, *Managing Quality: The Strategic and Competitive Edge* (New York: The Free Press, 1988). Schonberger points out that the four unstarred items are not just variations or extensions of the first eight: they are basic and vital in their own right. Thus quality, considered carefully, includes more than has been traditionally subsumed in the term, certainly much more than conformance to specifications. Conformance to specifications is desirable—essential—when the specifications are aimed at achieving customer satisfaction.

But even more, quality becomes everyone's job; it cannot be delegated to inspectors or a quality assurance department. This is where personal quality fits in. This seems like a blinding glimpse of the obvious, but it does need to be discussed, elaborated, and, above all, made concrete in terms of what we do from day to day.

Manufacturing Quality and Service Quality

Much of the work and literature on TQM has been focused on manufacturing. Quality in manufacturing requires meeting or exceeding customer expectations by making products that consistently operate within customer-based specifications.

Although manufacturing quality and service quality are similar— manufactured products are desired only to the extent that they provide services to customers—it is easier to understand and visualize good quality in manufacturing. People nod their heads in assent when they hear about service quality, but they don't know how to go about making it happen.

From manufacturing experience, we know that managing quality has two key components: to count and reduce defects; and to measure and reduce cycle time, the time that it takes to complete a given process, such as the assembly of a car. These fundamentals carry over to services. If you do not address these two fundamentals, you will *not* achieve your quality objectives. Do a good job on these fundamentals, and the rest is straightforward; it's fun. This requires, however, that every person in a service organization count defects or measure cycle time for those processes that are the most important in meeting or exceeding customers' expectations.

This sounds simple, but it demands a fundamental culture change in which customer expectations are accorded the highest importance, and ambitious goals are specified for improvement in all current processes. Note, in particular, that the easy answer of improving quality by hiring more people or spending more money becomes a last resort rather than a first step.

Service in the United States

Airplanes don't often take off and land on time, even in decent weather. When you get something repaired, it is likely that it won't be ready when promised, and that something else will be damaged in the process. If you need work done in your home or you expect a delivery to your home, prepare to rearrange your life for the convenience of the supplier. Salesclerks talk to each other and seem offended that you are interrupting them. There are lines to check in at hotels in the evening and then to check out in the morning. You may die in the hospital emergency room while they get the information you gave them three months ago; if you survive the emergency room and are admitted to the hospital, you will provide the same information again, perhaps many times.

Traditionally, these examples are typical of service levels. If customers have even thought about it, they have concluded that poor service, like death and taxes, is inevitable. The only option seems to be to grin and bear it.

But it doesn't have to be this way: things are changing. If you need next-morning delivery of a package from Chicago to Los Angeles, you can rely on Federal Express to get it there. If you want to have a wonderful vacation with your children or grandchildren, you know that you will have a great time at Disney World. If you need a customized pager the next day, you can bet on Motorola having it in your hands. It is possible for U.S. companies to provide outstanding service. Not many are doing it yet, but the number is increasing, and there are great opportunities for executives and managers who want to differentiate themselves—whether an entire company, a department, a work group, or an individual. It costs something to do so, but the payout on the investment can be enormous.

2. PERSONAL QUALITY

Now we come to *personal* quality, which relates these generalizations about TQM to you and to us.

Bob Galvin, formerly CEO of Motorola, has listed "The Welcome Heresies of Quality," in which he contrasts the "old testament" (ot) and the "New Truths" (NT). The first items on his list are:

ot: Quality control is an ordinary company and department responsibility

NT: *Quality improvement is not just an institutional assignment, it is a daily personal priority obligation*

Our aim is to elaborate Galvin's "New Truth."

Galvin made it plain that one key to implementing a strong quality program in any organization is *personal quality*. You cannot delegate the concept of quality. One of the basic tenets of leadership is that you don't ask others to do what you are not willing to do yourself. You will make progress faster by leading and showing the way than by drawing maps and telling folks where to go.

This book elaborates the personal quality journey. A major emphasis is on a tool called the *Personal Quality Checklist*, which is introduced in the next section. But we also go beyond checklists to consider other tools for achieving and improving personal quality.

3. PERSONAL QUALITY CHECKLISTS

The authors have taken Galvin's first "New Truth" at face value. Much of our discussion will be focused on a simple tool that we call the Personal Quality Checklist, which turns out not only to be useful for training about quality but to have astonishing potential for quickly improving general work effectiveness, and also for improving quality in everyday life outside the workplace.

We have tried the Personal Quality Checklist ourselves and have encouraged hundreds of others to try it. Most have been substantially helped in their work performance. For a few, the Personal Quality Checklist has done even more: it has proved to be a simple but powerful way to cope with chronic frustrations of job and daily living.

Many quality experts call not only for continuous improvement but for breakthroughs of performance. The Personal Quality Checklist is good for continuous improvement, but it also can lead to breakthroughs. *It is not just an instructional tool.* Fortunately, we do not have to ask you to take this claim on faith. If you follow the general approach outlined in Chapters 1 and 2, you can verify or refute it within a few days or at most a few weeks.

The Personal Quality Checklist has greatly improved the effectiveness of meetings in the Central Region of AT&T and aided in systematic quality training there. It has been useful in getting a fast start on several quality training programs at the University of Chicago, ranging from the campus MBA program to the Executive Program, quality training for staff, and even a special Quality Forum for senior managers who were interested in getting their companies started on the TQM journey.

The Personal Quality Checklist has also been received with interest by a number of audiences at short courses and seminars on quality. The checklist is something anyone can actually try out on short notice with minimal instruction, without preliminary organizational preparation, formation of teams, and provision of budgetary support.

Beyond the checklist itself, we have found that a personal perspective on quality strengthens the understanding of general principles of quality, including especially the ability to recognize and eliminate waste in all activities, the visualization of quality concepts such as Just-In-Time production, the understanding of the key role of customer satisfaction in quality improvement, and the use of simple tools of data analysis.

What's New About Personal Quality Checklists?

Later we show that the idea of personal quality checklists goes back at least to Benjamin Franklin, so clearly the idea did not originate with us. What we try to do is to illustrate the possibility of tying checklists closely with the TQM approach and to show how use of quality checklists can improve on what many people—including probably many readers—have been doing in a less systematic way.

The Personal Quality Checklist resembles in some ways the various schemes for time management, which entail systematic checklists of things to do. There are two differences: the Personal Quality Checklist is aimed at improvement by removal of system flaws, and it entails much less paperwork. However, the two approaches are not incompatible: Some users of the Personal Quality Checklist have included a standard, "Keeping my time management system up to date."

In the first three chapters of this book, we provide a detailed account of the Personal Quality Checklist, and we discuss contributions of personal quality to quality in general.

In Chapter 4, we discuss other routes to personal quality improvement, including routes based on detailed measurements rather than Personal Quality Checklists; use of other quality improvement tools; elimination of constraints; systematic approaches to the elimination of waste, Just-In-Time at the personal level; improving personal quality by benchmarking; inspection and personal quality; housekeeping for greater efficiency and reduction of waste; personal quality and athletics; personal health care; process mapping; simple questionnaires; personal vision/mission statements; personal process management; and statistical work sampling.

Chapter 5 goes beyond personal quality to survey Total Quality Management in organizations and to suggest how the personal approach can strengthen organizational efforts at the implementation of Total Quality Management.

The Conclusion gives a one-page summation of the message of the book.

The Appendix presents an elementary statistics tutorial based on data from personal quality checklists.

KEEPING TRACK OF "DEFECTS"

To begin a Personal Quality Checklist, you simply keep track of short-comings—we like to call them defects—in your key personal work processes. A variation on the approach is to keep track of cycle time. (Cycle time is the length of time it takes to go through a process once; for example, we may speak of the cycle time of order filling as the elapsed time from receipt of an order to its shipment.) The aim is to reduce both defects and cycle times for important personal processes.

Why Count Defects?

The word "defect" has a negative connotation for some people who would like to keep track of times we do things right rather than times we do things wrong. Fortunately, most of us do things right much more often than we do things wrong, so it is easier in practice to count the defects. Moreover, we can get positive satisfaction from avoiding defects—witness accident prevention programs that count days without accidents.

Others suggest keeping track of the ratio of total defects to total opportunities for defects. Although this means more record keeping, it is sometimes feasible; in most instances, however, we suggest opting for simplicity of record keeping. Also, there are instances in which the total opportunity for defects *cannot* be counted: for example, we can count accidents, but we can't count opportunities for accidents.

Some with a background in statistical process control know that precise measurements are more informative than defect counts. Thus we learn more if we record precisely how many seconds we were early or late for a meeting, or if we measure the exact cycle time to fill an order. In certain applications of statistical process control in manufacturing, we may measure a dimension rather than record simply whether the dimension is in or out of specification limits. Our emphasis on defect counts rather than quantitative measurements reflects the judgment that the simplicity of defect counts makes it possible for people to record defects when they would not take the time and trouble for measurements.

There are times when we take measurements in any event, and we would do well to record and analyze them. For example, someone who takes the personal quality approach to monitoring health will want to record actual blood pressure readings rather than simply monitoring whether they were above a certain warning level. Someone who is seriously trying to lose weight will want to record actual weights rather than simply checking a defect for weights above some goal. On Sergesketter's 190-pound limit (see below), however, simply recording higher readings as defects permits him to maintain his weight at a satisfactory level.

In Chapter 5 and in the Appendix we discuss approaches to personal quality based on measurements.

You cannot reduce the number of defects in your processes if you don't count them, and you cannot reduce cycle time if you don't measure it. Leaders who expect their associates to count defects and measure cycle time in order to provide quality service must show them the way. Service will improve a lot faster.

To get started on your Personal Quality Checklist, you must identify the processes you personally use to do your work. Almost everyone uses meetings, telephone calls, and correspondence in one way or another. Also, it is important for everyone to make a good appearance and to stay healthy. With these ideas in mind, in the spring of 1990, Sergesketter developed an initial checklist as a simple way to improve personal quality. Here is his initial list:

On time for meetings
Answer phone in two rings or less
Return phone calls same or next day
Respond to letters in five business days
Clean desk
Credenza: only same day paper
Never need a haircut
Shoes always shined
Clothes always pressed
Weight below 190 pounds
Exercise at least three times per week

Sergesketter then shared this list with his associates at AT&T and asked them to help him avoid defects. He also encouraged associates to start their own lists based on the work they did and what was most important to them. Many did just that, and they started to learn more about quality together.

Here is more information about Sergesketter's list:

1. *On time for meetings:* There is no distinction between major defects and minor defects. If you are one second late, that is a defect. (If you wish, you can count an additional defect for each minute or five minutes you're late.) Soon, everyone was on time for every meeting; in fact, most people arrived a few minutes early, so many meetings began before the scheduled time. Everyone was there for one 8:00 A.M. meeting by 7:50, and so the meeting started. It took nine minutes, and was over before it was scheduled to begin! The experience has been that meetings take one-third less time when they start promptly. The productivity improvement is enormous, and it costs nothing.

2. *Answer phone in two rings or less:* Actually, the aim is one or less. Research has shown that most people think that the phone should be answered in two rings. It was learned from AT&T manufacturing experience that the designed cycle time for a process must be one-half the targeted maximum in order to have essentially all actual times within the maximum. This gave a chance to teach a quality guideline in a form that could be easily understood and appreciated.

3. *Return phone calls the same or next business day:* This is common courtesy and most people think they do an excellent job here, until they start to record the defects. (An appropriate standard is to record an additional defect for each additional day that a call is not returned.)

4. *Respond to letters in five business days:* This one couldn't even be scored until date stamping was set up for all arriving correspondence. Then it took a couple of months to realize that it was necessary to design a process with mean response of 2.5 days to achieve near-100 percent response in five days.

5. *Clean desk,* and *Only same day paper on credenza:* Until you are in a "Just-In-Time" operation with your paper flow, you can't believe how much time you are wasting going through the same paper without taking any action. All the time spent in prioritizing is wasted. This is another of those productivity bonuses that cost virtually nothing!

6. *Never need a haircut:* You look in the mirror and see that you need a haircut (or your hair tipped) and it can be a week before you can arrange it in your schedule. Charge a defect for each day that you

look in the mirror and see an unkempt image! This leads you to think how to solve the problem. One solution is to get a haircut every other week. If you get a haircut before you need one, then you will never need one. (We were led to this insight from Disney World, where you never see a dirty window because they literally wash the windows before they get dirty. Prevention achieved through planning is the quality principle at work here.)

7. *Shoes always shined,* and *Clothes always pressed:* These are similar to the haircut category.

8. *Weight below 190 pounds:* (This is five pounds above what the charts say is the ideal weight for Sergesketter, who is 6' 5" tall.) One key to success is to manage caloric intake, which illustrates the quality principle that desired results are achieved by working on the processes that produce the results. (Phil Scanlan, quality vice president for AT&T, marks a defect any day he is over his target weight. On those days, he also marks a defect for any foods he eats that are high in fat or calorie content.)

9. *Exercise at least three times per week:* To achieve fitness in limited time, try the Royal Canadian Air Force (RCAF) exercises, which take 11 minutes a session for males (12 minutes for females) and require no special equipment; and they are graduated by age. The book explaining them is still in print. The RCAF exercises do, however, require high intensity. Less intensive alternatives that take a little longer are given in Ken Cooper's books *Aerobics* and *The New Aerobics.* Many other good fitness programs are available.

4. FIRST EXPERIENCES WITH A CHECKLIST

Sergesketter put his list into effect in April of 1990. Figure 1 is a time-series chart or run chart—defects plotted in time order—of the first 18 monthly totals:

No refined statistical analysis is needed to see the substantial drop in the number of defects, rapid at first, slowing more recently. (Here again is a quality lesson: When you intervene in a process to improve it, plot the performance data in time order. If the intervention was clearly successful, as here, you can see the results without formal statistical analysis.)

But there is more to the story than this simple statistical record. Re-

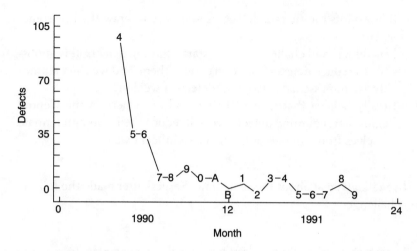

Figure 1   Number of Defects per Month Against Months

ducing defects is valuable only if the reduction leads to enhanced job performance. Here are some of Sergesketter's reactions as reported to his associates early in the process:

- ° I was not aware of the extent to which I was not returning phone calls the same or next day; this was a surprise to me.
- ° We had no way to count defects related to correspondence. As a result, we are starting to date stamp correspondence when it arrives and date stamp the file copy of the response.
- ° When you share your defect list with others, they will help you reduce defects.
- ° None of the items I measure is in the "four minute mile" category, and yet I started out at a rate of 100 defects per month.
- ° A 68 percent annual reduction of defect levels looks very attainable for what I am measuring.
- ° Some associates have asked about counting defects related to being on time for meetings. I will be late for a meeting rather than cut short a conversation with a customer, but I will count a defect. This has caused me to schedule my calls at times when the probability is low that I will be late for a meeting. If I notify people in advance that I will be late and specify the time I will be there, I do not count a defect unless I miss the specified time without further notification. Arriving for a meeting even one second after the scheduled starting

time counts for me as a defect, as you have to draw the line somewhere.

° I encourage and challenge you to start counting defects. It is impossible to reduce defects if we don't count them, and we can't reason-
ably ask our associates to count defects if we don't!

° I really believe that if several thousand of us here in the Central
Region start counting defects, we will reduce them and differentiate
ourselves from our competitors in a significant way.

In a talk given at about the same time, Sergesketter made the following challenge:

I want you to make a list of at least five areas that are important to you—
five things that will help you meet your personal and business needs—
and to count "defects," with your goal being 68 percent annual improvement.

Note that there was no requirement of a standard list, nor any attempt
to use the lists to grade employee performance.

Eighteen months later several interesting things had happened at the
Central Region of AT&T.

° Many employees now kept their own customized personal checklists. Here, for example, is the defect list of Diane Shank: meetings
on time; return all calls and audix within 24 hours; complete in-
basket in less than 24 hours; provide prompt feedback within 24
hours; answer all questions in five business days; take the train,
don't drive; practice music 15 minutes daily; don't eat chocolate;
answer phone in two rings.

° Employees liked to talk about their checklists and to help each
other to avoid defects.

° Meetings started on time, ended on time, and were much more
businesslike.

° Sergesketter estimated that this simple approach freed up over one
hour a day for him. This is suggestive for senior managers who believe that Total Quality Management is a good thing but can't find
time to lead TQM activities.

5. PERSONAL QUALITY CHECKLISTS
AND DEMING'S 14 POINTS

Dr. W. Edwards Deming has had enormous influence on the start and subsequent progress of what is sometimes called the "quality revolution." As a young man, he worked with Dr. Walter Shewhart of AT&T Bell Laboratories. (Dr. Shewhart was the creator of Statistical Process Control and the inventor of the control chart.) During the 1940s, Deming applied quality principles at the United States Bureau of the Census and taught many short courses in Statistical Process Control that had a substantial impact on the United States effort in World War II. In the 1950s, Deming—along with another American, Dr. Joseph M. Juran—was very influential in starting the thrust towards quality improvement in Japan that has become a target for the rest of the world to emulate. Widely recognized in the United States only for the last dozen or so years, he continues—in his early nineties—as an indefatigable and uncompromising advocate and teacher of quality methods for management.

Much of Deming's management philosophy is bound up in his famous 14 points, which he advocates as a route for transformation of management. We found it interesting to see how a Personal Quality Checklist can aid one to understand what Deming is driving at in these points. To our surprise, we were able to trace valuable connections with all of them.

Point 1: Create constancy of purpose toward improvement of product and service with the aim to become competitive and to stay in business and to provide jobs. A checklist, focused on key processes, creates a constant awareness of quality and demonstrates strong purpose towards continuous improvement.

Point 2: Adopt the new philosophy. We are in a new economic age. Western management must awaken to the challenge, must learn their responsibilities, and take on leadership for change. (See point 7 for comment.)

Point 3: Cease dependence on inspection to achieve quality. Eliminate the need for inspection on a mass basis by building quality into the product (service) in the first place. The best environment for reducing the need for final inspection arises when individuals are aware of, and responsible for the quality of, the processes by which they do their own work. The Personal Quality Checklist enables this environment.

Point 4: End the practice of awarding business on the basis of price tag. Instead, minimize total costs. Move toward a single supplier for any one item on a long-term relationship of loyalty and trust. The checklist concept can help to instruct suppliers on the principles of quality and assist in identifying those standards that need tracking. Suggestion of standards for the checklists of one's suppliers is an effective, tactful way to communicate requirements and to enable continuous improvement between customers and suppliers. In fact, exchange of checklist standards, with an invitation for suggested improvements, is a good way to improve almost any customer/supplier relationship, *including the all-important customer/supplier relationships within an organization.*

Point 5: Improve constantly and forever the system of production and service to improve quality and productivity and thus constantly decrease costs. Quality checklists enable continuous improvement by providing the data to the person doing the work. The information is immediate and credible. Because the person can add new standards as earlier ones come into control, a checklist facilitates progress both in quality and cost reduction.

Point 6: Institute training on the job. The Personal Quality Checklist can both aid in education and training and monitor the effectiveness of educational and self-improvement initiatives. The concept can be designed into educational and training materials, as we have done in a wide range of courses, including even MBA classes in quality management.

Point 7: Institute leadership. The aim of leadership should be to help people and machines and gadgets to do a better job. Leadership of management is in need of overhaul as well as leadership of production workers. As mentioned earlier, one of the tenets of leadership is that you don't ask the people you are leading to do what you are not willing to do yourself. Keeping a Personal Quality Checklist is visible and practical quality leadership. You will find it has a strong impact on your associates.

Point 8: Drive out fear so that everyone may work effectively for the company. All work is part of a process. Therefore the focus of managing processes rather than people is powerful and energizing to an organization. That focus drives out fear, because it is based on the premise that people basically want to do a good job and that when defects occur, the approach is not to fix blame but to fix the flawed process that led to the defects. People understand this concept quicker and better when they have personal experience with a Personal Quality Checklist for the processes they directly own. The checklist also helps to inculcate the idea that any process can be improved, which leads to open-minded consideration of suggestions for improvement from any associate.

Point 9: Break down barriers between departments. People in research, design, sales, and production must work as a team to foresee problems of production and use that may be encountered with the product or service. One of the most effective ways to break down barriers is to use data as opposed to anecdotes, perceptions, or intuitive insights. One difficulty, however, is that many people are either reluctant or don't know how to go about collecting data. The Personal Quality Checklist teaches a straightforward way to collect data. It takes the mystery out of how to do it. When people use data, it reduces and even eliminates the emotion that is often the root causes of barriers between departments.

Point 10: Eliminate slogans, exhortations, and targets for the work force asking for zero defects and new levels of productivity. With a focus on managing processes, it is no longer necessary to use slogans and exhortations to energize people. Defects become sources of information on how to improve quality. Continuous improvement follows. New levels of quality and productivity are achieved by reducing defects and reducing cycle time in the processes, not by setting broad objectives for the results of the processes. The rule is to keep your eye on the ball, not on the scoreboard. The Personal Quality Checklist brings this lesson home at the personal level.

Point 11a: Eliminate work standards (quotas) on the factory floor. Substitute leadership.

Point 11b: Eliminate management by objective. Eliminate management by numbers, numerical goals. Substitute leadership. The key is to manage processes, to focus on reducing defects and reducing cycle time. This requires strong leadership by people who can keep these fundamental principles foremost, and the Personal Quality Checklist facilitates such leadership—and facilitates acceptance of it.

Point 12a: Remove barriers that rob the hourly worker of his right to pride of workmanship. The responsibility of supervisors must be changed from sheer numbers to quality.

Point 12b: Remove barriers that rob people in management and in engineering of their right to pride of workmanship. This means inter alia abolishment of the annual or merit rating and of management by objective, management by the numbers. The abolition of merit ratings and traditional management by objective is the most difficult of Deming's concepts for many to

understand and accept. If you are managing people and not processes, traditional management by objective is the obvious tool for
driving alignment of the organization. However, that same approach also drives fear and intimidation into the organization and
destroys teamwork. If you start to apply the quality principles and
manage processes, you can drive out fear and build teamwork.
Again, keep your eye on the ball and not the scoreboard.

Point 13: Institute a vigorous program of education and self-improvement. On
Sergesketter's Personal Quality Checklist, he keeps a supplemental
record of number of days of education he has completed for the
year to date. His objective is a minimum of ten days of education
each year.

*Point 14: Put everybody in the company to work to accomplish the transformation.
The transformation is everybody's job.* The Personal Quality Checklist is
useful to everyone in the organization from the chief executive of-
ficer to the entry level clerk. It can put everybody to work, *overnight.*

6. HELP IN GETTING STARTED

We did not write this book on Personal Quality Checklists simply to
round out your general knowledge of ways to go about quality improvement. We have found that Personal Quality Checklists can be used with
effectiveness—including some very quick improvement—by almost everyone. In Chapters 2 and 3 we shall provide detailed guidance. Now we
give general guidance to help you get a quick start. We urge strongly
that you give the Personal Quality Checklist a try—*starting very soon!*

The key, as indicated in Sergesketter's example, is to keep track of
defects and cycle time on the most important standards of business and
personal life. The most important standard for an airline is that safe
landings equal takeoffs. You have to find your own standards. All busi-
nesses and individuals have to determine what is most important for
them. That is where to start.

A study of Fortune 1000 executives about service quality by the executive search firm, Paul Ray & Carre' Orban International, showed that
accuracy is considered to be the most important factor in determining
service quality; speed of response is a close second. Courtesy, ease of
access, and one-call resolution were also considered important.

To achieve accuracy and speed of response, it is essential to reduce the wastes—activities that can be altered or even eliminated without harm to performance—that pervade so much of what we do. Often these wastes are hidden, and we are not aware of them. In Chapter 4, we give hints on how to identify and reduce waste.

The Stroke Tally

Recording defects is much easier than quantitative measures often used in TQM; it takes just a stroke tally for each recognized defect. This tally is a simple and powerful tool. It promotes awareness, costs almost nothing, and yields accurate real-time data on one's personal work. *Each stroke is an opportunity to think about possible improvements.* The positive impact of the knowledge thus gained from a stroke tally can have a substantial bearing both on improvement of customer service and elimination of waste, two of the key routes to continuous improvement.

Often the lessons from the strokes leap off the tally sheet. In more complex situations, the strokes provide the input data for quality tools such as Pareto analysis, cause-and-effect diagrams, and run charts.

The Personal Quality Checklist provides a framework for people from all kinds of organizations, service as well as manufacturing, to form the habit of keeping stroke tallies. Once formed this useful and valuable habit can lead to formation of other good habits, for example, good habits about diet and exercise.

We shall talk also of approaches to quality based on measurements, rather than recording of defects. A measurement—say of actual cycle time—gives more information than a defect tally for failure to achieve a certain desired cycle time. But the simplicity of the stroke for a defect is a great practical advantage. It is well to become involved in detailed data collection and record keeping only when this is absolutely necessary.

Awareness

One of the keys to success and fulfillment in both our personal and professional lives is a heightened sense of awareness. It helps us to see the beauty of a flower, to appreciate the creativity embodied in a sonata, and to marvel at the taste of a dish prepared by a French chef. Awareness also helps us to see where we are wasting time, money, and resources in our work life, and where we are falling short of customer expectations.

The power of the simple stroke tally to heighten awareness is extraordinary. The strokes are facts, and facts are friends. They tell us what is really happening. When people start keeping a Personal Quality Checklist, they are usually amazed at what they learn about themselves from the stroke tally. This heightens awareness, which leads to insights about improvement. Habits quickly change for the better.

Any time you want to heighten your awareness, establish your standards and make a stroke on a card or piece of paper whenever a deviation—defect—occurs. You will be surprised and pleased at what happens.

Keep It Simple

You may think that the concept of a Personal Quality Checklist is too simple to be effective, that nothing so simple can deliver anything worthwhile. However, even in large organizations, simple systems are often far more effective in delivering top quality service than are more complex and expensive systems. Roger Dow, vice president of Marriott Hotels, tells three wonderful stories that illustrate this point.

> Roger checked into the Irvine, California, Marriott, and the desk clerk enthusiastically welcomed him back. He knew that they did not have any type of data base system for her to know that he had stayed there before, and that it had been several months since his last stay. He asked how long she had worked for Marriott, and she said one month. He was puzzled, so he asked her how she knew that he had stayed there before. She replied that the doorman, as they were walking to the desk, had asked him if he had previously stayed at this hotel. The doorman then tugged on his left earlobe to indicate that Roger had said yes. After the check-in process was complete, the young lady said: "Now watch this. Bellman, please show Mr. Dow to his room." As she said this, she tugged on her left earlobe. The bellman looked at Roger and said, "Mr. Dow, it's great to have you back. Let's go!"

> Roger had talked with the data processing organization about designing a system so that guests could have the morning paper of their choice delivered to their room. They said that they would look into it. The next week Roger checked into a Marriott Hotel in Miami and was asked

whether he would like *USA Today*, the *Wall Street Journal*, or the *Miami Herald* delivered to his room in the morning. He made his choice and then asked the desk clerk what system they were using to do this. She showed him a pad of blue-lined paper with three columns, one for each paper. Room numbers were placed under the appropriate column. At 2:00 A.M. the order was called in to the newspaper distributor, and the bellman used the list to distribute the papers. The next morning the paper Roger had requested was slipped under his door.

The head housekeeper at the Marriott Hotel on Michigan Avenue in downtown Chicago noticed that she was receiving a lot of calls requesting an ironing board and an iron. She took a stroke tally, and this type of call represented 64 percent of the total calls. Armed with this information, the housekeeping quality improvement team put together a purchase order for $25,000 to buy 1200 irons and ironing boards—one for every room. Having the facts from a simple stroke tally, the general manager was persuaded of the value of this proposal, but he didn't have an extra $25,000. However, he reviewed the capital program and saw an entry for $26,000 to be spent on replacing black and white television monitors with color television monitors in the bathrooms of the rooms on the concierge level. When the general manager spoke to the concierge, he learned that no guest had ever commented negatively (or in any way) about the television set in the bathroom. It was an easy decision. A simple process using some facts resulted not only in saving the housekeeper many calls, but eliminated scores of trips by bellmen and anxiety on the part of many guests who needed an iron right away.

"Keeping it simple" is often the most effective approach. This applies not only to service processes but to complex, even high-tech, manufacturing processes. One fine book on quality in manufacturing—*World Class Manufacturing*, by Richard J. Schonberger—is subtitled, *The Lessons of Simplicity Applied* (New York: The Free Press, 1986).

Recognition

An important part of Total Quality Management is recognition. In addition to recognizing groups for team efforts and successes, it is helpful to recognize individuals for their successes in personal quality. In the Central Region of AT&T, Gil Regnier started a recognition program in the Major Markets Area called "Lagniappe." Anyone in the area can nominate an associate for the Lagniappe Award when the associate is "caught in the act" of outstanding personal quality. The award is personalized so that it is something the person being recognized will particularly appreciate. One of the award recipients was a single parent with two small children. Gil arranged for someone to clean her house, which delighted her.

One of AT&T's branch managers in Chicago, Jim Burke, awards a special pin to associates who have demonstrated quality in their personal work in such a way that they prevent waste and rework. This award reinforces the quality principle that "Prevention Is Achieved Through Planning." The pin is worn with pride by those who have received it.

Both Gil and Jim were influenced by what they had seen and heard from others. Gil introduced his program after making a trip to visit Milliken in North Carolina and seeing a similar program. Jim formulated his plan after hearing Mike Vance talk about Walt Disney's philosophies about quality. Mike was responsible for training for Disney a few years ago and is a wonderful teacher. Bob Galvin talks about the importance of learning quality by studying what others are doing. Gil and Jim are great examples of people who have done this.

Voluntariness

Some managers become so enthusiastic about personal quality checklists that they are tempted to mandate their use among their subordinates. In our view, this is a mistake. Use of checklists should be encouraged by clear explanations of rationale and methods, and by examples of successful use, not by command.

7. PERSONAL QUALITY CHECKLISTS AND THE IMPLEMENTATION OF TQM

Implementation of ideas of TQM in organizations can be extraordinarily difficult. A few organizations have been very successful. Others bungle the job, and there are many ways to bungle. The most common problem is failure to understand that successful TQM requires the dedication of senior management to a transformation of organizational culture, which requires a shift from top-down control to widespread employee empowerment to make improvements. Employees must be recognized and rewarded, not punished, for making improvements. The key idea is Deming's eighth point: "Drive out fear," which includes fear of taking initiative to improve the way the organization works.

Another problem is faulty training. Organizations often start training programs for TQM with general awareness training, followed by specific instruction to prepare associates (employees) to work on quality improvement teams. These teams try to improve organizational processes, typically tackling messy interdepartmental problems for which solutions offer high payoffs.

Formation of improvement teams, however, is often slow. High-priority problems have to be identified, and teams have to be formed. Only after the first teams have achieved successes can formation of additional teams be accelerated. Hence before participating on a team, many trainees may find themselves marking time for months or even years after their initial training, during which time enthusiasm may cool and memories of the training grow hazy.

Personal Quality Checklists are a simple supplement to TQM training; indeed, they can often serve to "jump-start" a TQM program in an organization. As explained above, each individual must define desirable standards of personal job performance and then keep track of failures— "defects"—to meet these standards.

Each standard should have a clear relation to customer satisfaction. At the personal level, we have many customers. As members of an organization, the people in the organization who depend on our work are our (internal) customers, while all the customers of the organization itself are also our customers. Beyond our organizational customers, we have many other customers: for example, friends, family, neighbors, community, and nation. ("Ask what you can do for your country.")

Failure to keep customer satisfaction in mind often leads to discouragement in attempted implementations of TQM. Some companies work hard to make improvements that are of no importance to customers. For example, one company improved its on-time delivery record from about 40 percent to over 90 percent in a single year, only to find that it had lost market share. The problem was that its previous on-time record, while far from good on an absolute scale, was better than that of its competitors. In its preoccupation with improving its delivery record, the company neglected serious problems that did matter to its customers, such as providing prompt and timely response to customer questions, and competitors were doing a better job of that.

There are two broad types of standards; some standards may share aspects of each type.

1. Waste-reducers or time-savers; for example, "on-time to meetings and appointments" or "quick reply to phone messages and correspondence."
2. Activity-expanding activities; for example, "talk to all direct reports at least once per week" or "call parents at least twice a month."

The waste-reducers and time-savers help to develop a *personal* understanding of quality in terms of each employee's immediate work environment. This understanding is valuable in its own right, and it leads to more effective participation on improvement teams and other TQM activities.

One principle is essential: *The list must be balanced between waste-reducers and activity-expanders.* There must be enough waste-reducers to make time for the activity-expanders. Otherwise the checklist resembles a list of New Year's resolutions and quickly bogs down in a torrent of defects that cannot be easily corrected. Our experience suggests that ambitious exercise standards require more time than most people are likely to be able to find. Unless you really want to run a marathon, don't try to undertake an exercise program that would permit you to do so. Recall that Sergesketter does the RCAF exercises three times a week. The exercises take 11 minutes each day for a total of 33 minutes a week.

If you are in doubt, lean initially towards having too many waste-reducers. If you err in that direction, you can easily add activity-expanders later, but if you err in the direction of too many activity-expanders, you risk discouragement in the critical first days of your checklist.

A second principle is that all standards on your list—waste-reducers and activity-expanders—must be unambiguously defined so that you can recognize immediately when a defect occurs. You should never find yourself asking, "Should I count this as a defect?" Another way of saying this is that you must have *operational definitions* for all your standards. Operational definitions are essential for *all* measurements in TQM.

The Personal Quality Checklist plays more than a training role: it can bring immediate and substantial improvements in personal job performance, including typically the freeing of time to make it easier to participate in team improvement projects and other TQM activities. Moreover, since there is evidence of enormous waste in personal job performance, especially in service organizations, the aggregate effect of improvements in personal performance can itself be substantial. TQM can't be based on personal performance improvement alone, but improvement of personal performance can contribute greatly to TQM.

In this respect, Personal Quality Checklists can play the same role in TQM as a good suggestion system. In fact, the best Japanese suggestion systems—which elicit an average of one or more suggestions per week per employee—are directed mainly at improvements in the immediate workplace. They also include training in ways to recognize improvement opportunities.

Personal improvement efforts may pose a danger of "suboptimization." For example, an individual can increase numerical output by skipping steps or doing them in a sloppy fashion, thus exporting costs to the rest of the organization. This danger seems minimal for personal checklists because *reduction of waste* at the individual level can, in and of itself, do no harm. Of course, if the reduction of waste applies to an activity that does not contribute to the organization's goal, the reduction will do no good either, unless it frees up time for other value-adding activities. (One checklist user freed up a lot of time from several waste-reducers, but discovered that he had deteriorated on another waste-reducer—a limit on weekly viewing hours of television. His increased efficiency was thus wasted. Even in this example, however, he did no outright harm and presumably enjoyed the extra TV viewing!)

8. GROUP USE OF PERSONAL QUALITY CHECKLISTS

The Personal Quality Checklist is primarily an individual quality tool. It helps the individual better to serve internal and external customers, and thus to improve organizational performance. But, as in the example of improved meetings at AT&T because of the "on-time-to-meetings" standard, associates can help each other in meeting checklist standards with consequent improvement of group performance.

In some instances, small teams of employees—the equivalent of "quality circles"—have made shared checklists the basis of local improvement efforts. Members of the team help each other in setting up the standards in the first place and then meet periodically to identify problem areas. These meetings can be a catalyst for discussion of broader quality problems facing the team.

Letting Other People Keep Score

Professor Jay Shah has furnished this thought-provoking story about a novel group application. A checklist user was under heavy job stress and found himself grouching and snapping at his wife and children at the dinner table and around the house. He told them that he realized the problem and had decided to add a "snapping standard" to his checklist, but they noticed only moderate improvement. The children decided to post his new standard on the wall, and *they* took over the scoring of his defects. At the latest report, this step seems to have solved the problem.

2

HOW TO GET STARTED ON YOUR OWN PERSONAL QUALITY CHECKLIST

The Personal Quality Checklist is such a simple idea that you may well be skeptical about its potential benefits. As we pointed out in Chapter 1, you have to try it yourself. After learning of Sergesketter's experiences at AT&T, Roberts did so. He was surprised by how much and how quickly the list began to help. On the first day, he noticed an improvement in general ability to cope with his job, an improvement that has been maintained for a year in the face of increasing job pressures.

Although "clean desk" was not an explicit standard on his list, his desk went from cluttered to clean in just one week, much to the shock of his associates. We will explain in a moment how this came about.

It is important to approach a checklist with ambitious goals in mind. Moreover, as one student checklist user, Tamara Kelling, put it, "If modest goals are set, the tendency is to think, 'I'll just do it better.' When very aggressive goals are set, I tend to think, 'I'd better do it differently.'" "Doing it differently" means that she was removing constraints, and removal of constraints has been seen in Chapter 1 to be a key idea of Total Quality Management.

1. DRAWING UP THE CHECKLIST

The hardest part is drawing up the checklist itself. The actual data collection is almost effortless. As we have explained, you just tally defects by stroke marks when defects are noticed. It is very tempting to develop a more elaborate system that entails more record keeping; unfortunately such systems add little value and tend to bog down from the recording burden.

The key to success is devising a good checklist. This requires some

27

insight into one's own job function and some knowledge of TQM principles; we explain many of these principles in this book.

By describing his own efforts in some detail, Roberts—a professor—can give tips that may help readers to get started quickly and successfully. A professor's job functions are not like the popular stereotypes. A substantial amount of time is spent in activities that will be familiar to managers, clerical employees, professionals, even students. These activities resemble Sergesketter's: processing incoming written and oral information and going to meetings. The diversity of incoming tasks is high. Most of these tasks can be done very quickly, and it is a principle of TQM that the quicker they are done, the better. If they are delayed, they clog up the system.

Roberts had excellent qualifications to be a guinea pig for personal quality checklists: He had long been a walking laboratory of poor job habits. But from his background in TQM, he knew that attempting to work harder and faster or to install a completely new personal work system (including, for example, a computerized filing system) would probably be counterproductive. He knew also that the surest route to improvement was to eliminate wastes, obvious and nonobvious, in all their forms. (Training in the identification and elimination of waste is essential to the success of the personal checklist; this will be discussed in Chapter 4.)

2. THE INITIAL CHECKLIST

After careful self-observation and reflection over two or three weeks, Roberts assembled a list of seven standards, some borrowed from Sergesketter, which are shown blow in the accompanying table.

Harry Roberts's Personal Quality Checklist: Week of_____

Defect Category	Mon	Tue	Wed	Thu	Fri	Sat	Sun	Total
Late for meeting or appointment								
Search for something misplaced or lost								
Delayed return of phone call or reply to letter								

Defect Category	Mon	Tue	Wed	Thu	Fri	Sat	Sun	Total
Putting a small task in a "Hold pile"								
Failure to discard incoming junk promptly								
Missing a chance to clean up junk in office								
Unnecessary inspection								
Total								

Comments:

With his checklist, Roberts included a list of definitions and explanations, that were printed, for reference, on the backside of the list itself.

> *Late for meeting or appointment:* Late by even one second. Always carry background reading or work materials in case others are late.
>
> *Search for something misplaced or lost:* More than momentary confusion as to location of important document, book, address, working materials, etc. Forgetting a task or working material is included here.
>
> *Delayed return of phone call or reply to letter:* Failure to act at the first opportunity. Note: Even if a lengthy reply to a letter will eventually be needed, a short acknowledgment should be made immediately.
>
> *Putting a small task in the "hold pile" when it can be done quickly now:* A hold pile (work in process) seems unavoidable but must be kept small and attacked continually. Note: One important "small task" is filing.
>
> *Failure to discard incoming junk promptly:* Failure to act on first reading or skimming of written materials. In case of doubt, have a "hold-in-case pile" that is periodically screened and discarded.
>
> *Missing a chance to clean up junk in office:* I suffer from decades of accumulated junk. Given persistence, much can be done to throw out junk.
>
> *Unnecessary inspection:* Checking something I've probably already done but didn't pay attention when I did it.

Notice that defects are tallied by days, not by weeks or months. In that way, progress can be followed closely from the first day to see quickly whether or not improvement is occurring. Later, the data may be aggregated by weeks or months for long-term monitoring.

There is another benefit in daily tabulation: If personal quality check-lists are used for TQM training, each participant will quickly have a substantial series of personal data to illustrate elementary TQM statistical tools such as run charts and Pareto diagrams. The data can also be used for simple time-series analysis, such as fitting of trends and day-of-week effects, if these are within the scope of the training program.

3. INITIAL EXPERIENCES

Roberts started on Monday, 30 September 1991. During the first week, he accumulated seven defects: five for "search for something lost or misplaced" and two for "unnecessary inspection." That was not surprising; if anything, an even poorer performance had been expected.

What was surprising was that there were *no defects at all on any of the other five standards*. Did this mean that these five standards were unnecessary? The answer to this question gives a surprising insight: a well-constructed personal quality checklist *can give an immediate improvement that is not actually measured*. This can be called an "instant triumph."

This happened as follows. If, unbeknown to Roberts, a guardian angel had been keeping track of defects in these five standards *before* he started his checklist, there would have been *many* defects in these five standards. But once the checklist was in his pocket, there was a remarkable change of behavior. The list was a continuing reminder of new standards that had to be satisfied or defects would be recorded. He realized that with a little effort, he could literally *prevent* most defects in these standards.

The checklist was an almost magical device that calmed him down, made him resist the temptation to try to do everything at once, shuffle madly to find what to do next, and in general create chaos on the desk. As reported above, during the first week, the desk went from cluttered to clean. (Roberts would almost rather eat glass than let it start to get cluttered again.)

The key checklist standard in this accomplishment was "Putting a small task in a 'hold pile.'"

In the terminology of Joseph M. Juran, a leading quality authority, the five standards for which no defects were incurred during the first week were largely "operator controllable." By contrast, the "lost or misplaced" standard is not completely controlled by the operator. Roberts's underlying filing systems are bad: poor organization and filing will take a long time to correct, and defects will continue. (The standard "Missing a chance to clean up junk in the office" is a recognition that one route to improvement of filing systems is to get rid of unneeded materials.)

"Unnecessary inspection" is also not completely operator controllable. Roberts suffers from the absentmindedness or inattention that is supposed to be characteristic of professors, but is not unknown for others; it seems to get worse with age for everyone. One way to cope with absentmindedness is a kind of "mistake-proofing": Talk to yourself when doing an important task; for example, "I am putting this folder in George Bateman's mailbox." The incurrence of a defect on "unnecessary inspection" serves as a reminder *to talk to yourself when putting anything down, even temporarily.*

Mistake-proofing is an important TQM tool. It prevents someone, for example, from putting leaded gas into the tank of a car designed to run only on nonleaded gas. Mechanical and electronic mistake-proofing tools are common in manufacturing; we need to think of counterparts that work for service activities. It is harder in service activities precisely because of the problem of inattention. For a personal example of mistake-proofing, consider a standard that is especially important to many students: getting up early in the morning. A common temptation is to hit the snooze alarm, perhaps repeatedly. Several students have licked that problem by the simple expedient of putting the alarm clock across the room!

Thus Roberts's list had a calming effect that led to the gratifying, though unmeasured, improvement in week one. After the first week, total weekly defects trended downward, more rapidly at first, then more slowly. At this writing, a year later, some standards are still hard. "On time to meetings and appointments" brings occasional defects as special, noncontrollable causes—a last-minute phone call or a question asked by a student encountered on the way to the meeting—occur. The poor filing system, only slightly improved during a year, still causes "search for something lost or misplaced."

But the gains are substantial. They have been welcomed especially because during this same one-year period job demands sharply increased; in the absence of the list, a general collapse might have occurred. And gains are not measured solely in defect reduction. The existence of such a list can stimulate people to watch their own working behavior—the theme of "awareness" again—to notice inefficiencies that are not directly covered in any of their checklist standards. Improvement in one standard "drives" improvement in others.

These details on Roberts's experience are provided mainly as an illustration of the kind of thinking that should go into the construction of a Personal Quality Checklist. He has found that many people seem to identify with his problems and difficulties; the cluttered desk syndrome is not uncommon! One faculty colleague even said the list could almost have been made for him. The many students who have now done self-improvement projects based on checklists have found a number of Roberts's (and Sergesketter's) standards to be useful. They have also added many other standards of their own; these will be discussed later.

Cautions

Two important cautions, mentioned in Chapter 1, deserve repetition:

1. Each standard must be unambiguously defined, so that you can recognize a defect when it occurs. (This illustrates the importance of operational definitions, stressed by Deming as indispensable for all quality measurements.)
2. If you include activity-expanders on your list, be sure that you will have enough waste-reducers and time-savers to open up free time for them. Don't just make a New Year's type resolution that you will do additional tasks by sheer willpower. (Another quality principle: For improvement, don't place primary reliance on trying harder. As Deming would say, you are probably already trying very hard to do your best. As Tamara Kelling, a student, would put it, don't try harder to do what you're already doing; figure out a different way to reach the objective.)

4. ADDITIONAL CHECKLIST STANDARDS

Here, for your consideration, are additional checklist standards that were considered by Roberts but, for various reasons, not used. (Experience suggests that overly long checklists are unwieldy. A rule of thumb is no more than ten standards for work processes. Sergesketter's checklist had eleven standards, but only six applied to work processes.

Unnecessary shuttling of working materials between home and office: Commuters who do some work at home pay a price for maintaining two offices.

Failure to meet target dates for major projects.

Failure to listen carefully: Useful, but has to be defined carefully so that defects can be recognized when they occur.

Failure to devote time to long-term improvement activities: These could include background reading and study, enhancement of computer capabilities, etc.

Failure to recover promptly from interruptions: Falling into dazed paper shuffling when the interruption ends. Cleaning up office junk is one way to recover from the shock of an interruption, but it is desirable to get back quickly to what you were doing when the interruption struck. One key is to convince oneself that interruptions are inevitable, not deliberate acts of torture.

Personal fitness lapses: A very popular standard for many who have tried the checklist approach. Warning: Don't set overly ambitious targets, especially if you are starting from zero or a low base.

Procrastination: Letting unimportant immediate tasks be an excuse for postponing longer term projects, especially unpleasant projects. This standard does pose tricky problems of definition: How does one actually recognize when a particular act of procrastination has occurred?

Miscellaneous defects: Misdialing phone numbers, typos in manuscripts, failure to make notes of things to do or of names and phone numbers, failure to consult one's calendar, misfiling, etc.

Further standards are given below and in the case histories at the end of Chapter 3.

As mentioned earlier, improvement on one's basic standards may also "drive" improvement in areas not covered on the checklist itself. Roberts has the impression, for example, that he is recovering more promptly from interruptions, misdialing fewer phone numbers, and so on. There is a general TQM principle operating here: Improvements in measured activities will tend to drive improvements in similar or related activities that are not being measured.

It is important to feel free to modify an initial personal checklist in the light of experience. Statistical continuity over time is obtained so long as some of the defect standards are retained. But individual additions and subtractions may be desirable. *Like everything else, the Personal Quality Checklist should be subject to continuous improvement.*

Indeed, some users have found that the standards on their checklists become so ingrained that very few defects are incurred, and they discontinue the initial checklist, finding that they have no trouble meeting the standards. Then they switch either to a new checklist, or to some of the other routes to quality improvement that do not rely on the checklist approach at all; some of these routes are outlined in chapter 4.

A Promising but Difficult Standard: "Loss of Concentration"

One interesting standard deals with "loss of concentration" in reading, listening, or execution of routine tasks. Potentially such a standard could lead to very large gains in personal performance, but it is hard to define the standard operationally. The problem is that you may lose your concentration in keeping track of your losses of concentration. Even if you were able to record all your lapses, you might end up spending too much time tallying and adding up tally points, because for many of us, woolgathering, daydreaming, or just thinking seriously about something else are very common occurrences. (At times—say when you have to sit through a poor talk or dull meeting—lapses may even be desirable!)

Here is one possible way to deal with this opportunity:

- ° Define carefully the activities on which you are going to focus your efforts in enhancing concentration.
- ° Whenever you are aware of a lapse of concentration in these activities, don't try to tally a defect but focus brief attention on ways of preventing a recurrence.
- ° At the end of each day, score your efforts for the day on a quantitative self-evaluation scale—say from one point for very poor concentration to five points for very good concentration. This is similar to the self-evaluations of mood made by patients of depression.
- ° Make this a separate project or subproject from your basic checklist.
- ° If later you find that you are having few lapses of concentration and are aware of the ones that occur, you can add this standard to your basic checklist and simply count defects.

We offer further discussion along these lines in Section 13 of Chapter 4.

Checklist Standards for Students

The standards listed above have proven useful for many who are getting started on their own checklists, but the success of a checklist depends very much on the selection of standards that are most helpful for each person. We have found, for example, that students have thought of useful standards that nonstudents would not so readily come up with. The following standards were developed by MBA students.

- Review class notes after each class meeting.
- Keep personal phone calls to a maximum of ten minutes whenever I am in control of the situation.
- No more than ten hours a week in television viewing.
- Out of bed promptly; don't rely on snooze alarm.
- All assigned reading done before each class.
- Make a brief outline plan for what is to be accomplished each day. (The time-management approach.)
- Refer to this plan each day.
- Use stairs instead of elevators when feasible.
- Follow up job contacts within 24 hours.
- Work in library to avoid interruptions.
- Stick to one subject when studying; don't hop around.
- Don't doggedly persist in trying to clear up confusion when really stuck; get help, or set the point aside and come back to it later.
- Don't spend too much time on certain activities; for example, no more than 15 minutes on breakfast.
- Remember names of people to whom you have been introduced recently. (Systematic memory systems can help with this one.)
- In bed every night before midnight.
- Good housekeeping standards around room, apartment, or house.
- Prompt payment of bills.
- Various dietary standards, such as eating fruits and vegetables or avoidance of fats.
- Limitations on beer drinking or cigarette consumption. (Some students have made progress towards complete elimination of smoking.)

The "job" of student presents more of a challenge for personal quality than do most jobs in business. Experience with student checklists reflects increasing emphasis on one theme: punctuality in reviewing notes on lectures, keeping current on readings, and holding to schedule on assignments. Students since time immemorial have tended to get behind on course work and try to make it up by a sprint at the end. By introducing various aspects of punctuality on their checklists, today's students can help to end this discouraging tradition. By saving waste and time, students can add substantial value.

We have said that "procrastination" is a hard standard to define operationally. The suggestions in the previous paragraph illustrate one way to do so: You identify individual events that define whether or not you procrastinate, such as timely completion of readings and course assignments; then count defects on these.

Another useful standard that applies to us all, but perhaps especially to students, deals with "housekeeping" in both the narrow and broad sense. Canon has a major program in improving housekeeping, the Five S Program; it is essentially designed to reduce waste time in looking for working materials and to make the working environment safer (see Chapter 4, Section 8). Although Canon uses the system as an organizational tool, the basic idea is that there should be a place for all working materials, and all materials should be in that place when they are not in active use.

5. BENJAMIN FRANKLIN'S PRECEDENT: IMPROVING CHARACTER AND BEHAVIOR

Recall that five of the eleven standards on Sergesketter's original checklist were not *directly* business-related: never need a haircut; shoes always shined; clothes always pressed; weight below 190 pounds; and exercise at least three times a week. We have found that most people want a few such standards. Exercise and fitness are the most popular, but there are many others. One of the most interesting, which many people elect, is aimed at avoiding the use of profanity!

Thus the Personal Quality Checklist has potential even outside the world of business and organizations. As Benjamin Franklin reported in his *Autobiography* over two hundred years ago, the same approach can be used to improve a person's character and behavior. Franklin's 13 standards were: temperance, silence, order, resolution, frugality, industry, sincerity, justice, moderation, cleanliness, tranquillity, chastity (or "venery"), and humility. He reported overall satisfaction with results, but admitted some failures. "In truth, I found myself incorrigible with respect to Order; and now I am grown old and my memory bad, I feel very sensibly the want of it." Order, of course, is an essential ingredient of a personal quality checklist even for business.

Franklin also found humility to be hard: "In reality, there is, perhaps, no one of our natural passions so hard to subdue as *pride*. . . . Even if I could conceive that I had completely overcome it, I should probably be proud of my humility."

Inspired by Benjamin Franklin, Roberts made a second checklist to try to improve character and behavior. His aim was less ambitious and more specific than Franklin's. The seven headings are: (1) *Flustering*: getting rattled under pressure, (2) *Griping*: blaming others (including Congress or the President) when something goes wrong; (3) *Unpleasantness*: making irritation or frustration obvious by the way one talks or acts; (4) *Worry* that is not directed towards doing something about the object of worry; (5) *Defeatism*: depression, discouragement, and gloominess; (6) *Driving lapses*: mental lapses, usually minor but worrisome, even though they have thus far never resulted in an accident; (7) *Unkind humor*.

Unpleasantness was inserted because Roberts realized that he often replied in an irritated tone of voice when his wife asked him to so something that he was about to do anyway. It has worked pretty well; his wife, also, has improved by not asking him to do so many of those things he was about to do. (She knows of the checklist.)

One might think that a mere checklist couldn't cope with character and behavioral problems, especially discouragement, or depression; or that it even might make them worse. Roberts's experience and that of a number of his students give grounds for thinking otherwise. If the checklist is firmly embedded in one's consciousness, the threat of a defect is a surprisingly strong deterrent to undesirable behavior, even apparently uncontrollable behavior. One student with a lifelong problem of speeding has reported major improvement by including "speeding" as a standard on his list. Roberts knows of several instances in which exchange of checklists has helped to smooth over frictions in working relations. (Here is another important quality principle: It is almost always useful to learn more about what one's customers prefer.)

Surprisingly, the calming effect of the list was even stronger for Roberts's "character and behavior" list than for his business checklist. His defect level started and has continued very low. He was amazed to find that even such standards as "defeatism" are, to a degree at least, controllable. If he notices that he is starting to feel sorry for himself, he immediately rejects the feeling and does or thinks about something else, thus staving off a defect.

Franklin's Successive Focusing

Benjamin Franklin had one interesting variation on the approach we have been suggesting, a variation that may be useful to many.

> I determined to give a week's strict attention to each of the virtues successively. Thus, in the first week, my great guard was to avoid every day the least offence against *Temperance*, leaving the other virtues to their ordinary chance, only marking every evening the faults of the day. Thus, if in the first week I could keep my first line, marked T, clear of spots [tally strokes], I suppos'd the habit of that virtue so much strengthen'd, and its opposite weaken'd, that I might venture extending my attention to include the next, and for the following week keep both lines clear of spots. Proceeding thus to the last, I could go thro' a course compleat in thirteen weeks, and four courses in a year. And like him who, having a garden to weed, does not attempt to eradicate all the bad herbs at once, which would exceed his reach and his strength, but works on one of the beds at a time, and, having accomplish'd the first, proceeds to a second, so I should have, I hoped, the encouraging pleasure of seeing on my pages the progress I had made in virtue, by clearing successively my lines of their spots, till in the end, by a number of courses, I should be happy in viewing a clean book, after a thirteen weeks' daily examination.

6. HOW TO LEARN FROM DEFECTS

As we pointed out in Chapter 1, some people find the word "defect" objectionable; they don't like the negative sound. As Roberts and Sergesketter used their checklists, however, they found that defects were valuable friends, because each one suggested an opportunity for improvement. This happens because for each defect, one asks "Why did it occur?" and "How can a recurrence be prevented?" And the "why" and "how" questions are asked repeatedly, in the spirit of the Japanese "Five Whys." The repeated whys bring one closer to root causes and thus to possible remedies. The repeated "hows" lead one closer to satisfactory remedies. The aim is insight into ways of improving the system.

For example, suppose that a letter is misplaced in your office and later found on a filing cabinet. The following dialogue with yourself ensues:

"Why did you misplace the letter?" "Because I absentmindedly set it down on the filing cabinet and forgot where I put it."

"Why did you have the letter by the filing cabinet?" "Because I was interrupted by a phone call that required me to go over to the filing cabinet, and I took the letter with me."

"Why did you take the letter with you?" "Because I had it in hand when I answered the phone, and continued to read it while talking on the phone."

"Why did you set the letter down on the file cabinet?" "It was awkward to open the file drawer while holding the letter."

"Why didn't you pick up the letter when you returned to your desk?" "I forgot."

"Why did you forget?" "I was thinking about the phone call."

"Why didn't you set the letter down on the workspace on your desk before going over to the file cabinet?" "I was distracted by the phone call."

"Why were you distracted by the phone call?" "I easily get upset by interruptions. There are so many of them that I have trouble getting anything done."

The "whys" lead to "hows": "How can you cope better with interruptions?" "How can you remember where you set things down?" "How can you train yourself to put down objects in a logical place when you have to do something else?" These "hows," in turn, suggest possible routes toward improvement. Some of these routes are "workarounds" rather than long-term solutions, but even workarounds are helpful until the long-term solutions evolve.

For example, you might reconsider your habit of reading something unrelated to the subject of phone calls while talking on the phone. You might consider a policy of putting down current working materials in a designated work space on your desk whenever you have to switch tasks. In turn, this may cause you to think about better ways to use desk space when it is necessary to work on more than a single task. Further, you might address the problem of letting interruptions throw you off stride. This isn't easy, but it's essential.

An anecdote may help to suggest how to approach interruptions. Once Roberts shared an office and telephone with Professor Murray Rosenblatt. Their office telephone extension was changed to 2756, the former phone number of Student Health Service. The new health service number was 2656. As a result, Roberts's and Rosenblatt's phone rang constantly. Rosenblatt was so irritated by this that when he heard the request for Student Health Service, he would hang up—usually violently. This didn't help; the phone would immediately ring again. Roberts found a simple reply that dealt with the problem: "You want 2656, not 2756. That's the new number of Student Health Service." Initially this didn't help Rosenblatt because he was so upset that he was unable even to recall the number 2656. Finally, "2656" was written in large letters on the blackboard.

7. SHOULD ONE AIM FOR PERFECTION?

An interesting question is how long to try to keep driving down personal defects. One philosophy is that one never stops driving down defects, no matter how rare they become: the aim is always perfection. Keep on reducing defect numbers by, say, 68 percent a year, which means reducing them by a factor of 10 every two years.

There's a lot to be said for that philosophy. If your main job is centered on a particular process, you should continue to seek further reduction of error rates (or of cycle times) on that process, no matter how good you have become. After all, you are going to be spending a lot of time on that process anyway, because it is your main job.

But personal checklists deal with many processes, and overzealous efforts on one process may detract from more sorely needed improvements on other processes. Moreover, there are other problems in seeking perfection on any particular personal process:

1. Some defect standards are not completely controllable by the individual. "Late to meetings" is a good example.
2. Even with the best of efforts, the limits of human attention may prevent complete elimination of certain kinds of errors. Accidents are a good illustration.

(Error rates like three per million in manufacturing are usually achieved by mistake-proofing and automation. Although there is some room for both mistake-proofing and automation in personal quality performance, we have seen that this room is limited by human inattention and the influence of extraneous events. It would be surprising, for example, if anyone could achieve an error rate even as low as 1000 per million in dialing correct phone numbers. We have tried!)

3. Your first Personal Quality Checklist should focus on improving what you are currently doing. You will see your habits change and your personal productivity will improve. When you determine that the processes you are tracking are under control at an excellent level, it is time to add some items in the spirit of continuous improvement. You will still want to hold the gains from your current checklist, but it is easy to record the few defects that are still occurring, thus reminding yourself of the need to avoid complacency.

Now is the time to seek input from your associates and your family. Sergesketter has recently expanded his checklist after two years of experience with the original one. He solicited advice from associates as to desirable new standards, and gave a copy of the proposed list to his wife.

Your revised list will include areas for improvement that had not occurred to you before. Don't add too many items, as you never want the list to become a burden. Think of the list as a friend who can make you more aware. Remember that each defect provides you with information that you may have overlooked. You would almost certainly not be aware of the pattern of the defects you record without keeping the list. More broadly, the checklist itself should be subject to continuous improvement.

One way to look at it is this. The standards on any checklist are likely to include only a small fraction of one's activities. For example, "On time for meetings" says nothing in itself about what one does in the meetings. It seems that being on time to meetings indirectly contributes to a state of mind that leads to improved participation in meetings. But participation may be made more effective by a new standard that deals with behavior at meetings; for example, not disparaging anything said by other participants or not making one's own point in a tactless way or remembering to bring all essential background materials to the meeting.

In addition to expansion of the checklist, you may also want to consider other, more elaborate, types of personal improvement projects that go beyond checklists. For example, even if you aren't up to an overhaul of your filing system, you may look at ways of improving the filing of current materials for ready retrieval. Chapter 4 may give you other useful ideas along these lines.

Neurotic Perfectionism

When we talk about "aiming for perfection," we mean "perfection" in the eyes of the customer. There is a danger that the word "perfection" can be perverted to become compulsive attention to details that do not matter to customers, which we term "neurotic perfectionism."

Most of us are far from any kind of perfection, sane or neurotic, but there is a real danger in some aspects of our behavior. For example, the authors have observed that every time we reread this manuscript, we make changes, minor and major. That is to be expected from the idea of continuous improvement. Obviously, however, we have to stop at some point, or the book would never get finished. You may find similar temptations to neurotic perfectionism in some aspects of your own work.

One important organizational TQM application of this idea is in new product development. Successful product development projects usually have provision for a cutoff date beyond which further changes will have to be deferred to the next new product generation.

---

8. DEALING WITH DISCOURAGEMENTS

Most users of well-thought-out checklists attain substantial improvement at the start, and improvement continues for a long time before flattening out. But this is not always so.

For example, in an MBA class in TQM, some of the students made substantial improvements early in the term, but then lost a little ground at the end. Needless to say, this was puzzling and even upsetting. The main problem was that job interviewing activities became very intense late in the term. Students who have a lot of job interviews have less time to meet other standards, such as exercise or reviewing class notes.

To deal with such problems, it is a good idea to keep some auxiliary records on external requirements that may affect your ability to meet checklist standards. For example, students could keep track of the numbers of job-seeking letters and phone calls and actual job interviews. Then if defects increase but external demands are obviously intensifying at the same time, they can avoid unnecessary discouragement or self-blame. (Those who have some capability to do statistical analysis can use this information to check out whether the rise in defects is "explained" by the rise in external demands.)

Other frequent causes of setbacks are illness, injury, family emergencies, and increased job demands. They can be dealt with in the same way.

Occasionally, even with a good checklist, there will be no initial improvement at all. This may reflect an individual's severe overcommitment that cannot be easily overcome, even with substantial improvements in personal quality. In at least one instance, a frustrating experience with a checklist made overcommitment obvious for the first time, and the individual faced up to a major cutback in commitments.

Finally, it should be remembered that—as with Roberts—a checklist often leads to an unmeasured but real and substantial improvement at the very start. Slow progress thereafter must be interpreted in light of that initial gain.

Some Standards May Be Imperfect

Sometimes people find that they continue to get defects on a particular standard, almost regardless of what they do. This may happen because the standard is only a pious hope that they never really had their hearts set on. Consider a smoker who, *thinking* she really wants to stop smoking, charges one defect for each cigarette smoked. No improvement occurs, and it's even hard to keep track of the defects. In these circumstances, the problem may be a deep psychological problem that cannot be dealt with by a checklist. The nonsmoking standard should simply be removed from the list and dealt with separately. It should not interfere with progress on other checklist standards.

Another, less serious example, has come up with respect to the use of profanity. The problem again is that though the individual thought that eliminating profanity was desirable, he really enjoyed indulging in foul language and didn't actually believe it to be a very serious failing.

However, a number of checklist users have made progress on breaking such habits as smoking and profanity. One even appears to have broken a serious drinking problem. It depends on the individual.

3

EXPERIENCES WITH PERSONAL QUALITY CHECKLISTS

We have now had extensive experience in helping others to develop and implement checklists. The AT&T experiences came first and have already been reported. The first university test case was a class of 81 students in a course in statistics and quality management of the Executive Program, Graduate School of Business, University of Chicago. Students in the Executive Program class evaluated a project based on the Personal Quality Checklist even more highly than an organizational improvement project that was also required.

The Executive Program experience has been confirmed by subsequent MBA classes, in a special Total Quality Management training course for administrative staff at the University of Chicago, by a special TQM course for CEOs of small and medium-sized companies, and by the testimonials of many to whom our original report has been circulated. We have also had good results in presenting the basics of checklists in talks at meetings and short courses.

All this experience has been encouraging. Although it was introduced primarily as an educational tool, the Personal Quality Checklist has turned out to be an important event in the lives of many students. Some felt that it helped to gain control of a job that had trapped them into a cycle of overwork and frustration. Others have seen it as a key to improvement of their organizations. Tink Campbell, president of Goodman Equipment Corporation and a good friend of the authors, was not immediately convinced by us to try the approach. After reading a draft of this book, he reported, "I have been thinking about doing this for the last year, and now I have done it—with conviction. By measuring defects, improvements are already evident which I am convinced will help me personally and my business by creating positive effects on others' productivity. My list attempts to balance value adders with waste reducers. I anticipate that resistance to change in my company will weaken and we will develop an ever-increasing customer orientation."

We include Personal Quality Checklists at the first session of TQM courses and training programs. And we get the students started immediately on *doing it*. This eliminates the lag that typically occurs between TQM training and actual experience in TQM application, a lag that sometimes results in forgetting and loss of enthusiasm.

Personal improvements from the checklists have come from two expected sources:

1. An initial calming effect of having the checklist in one's pocket. (Delores Conway of the University of Southern California suggests calling this a "transfer effect," a debundling that permits action without introspection, that harnesses motivation.)
2. Continuing improvement as the list is maintained over time, progress is monitored, and defects are studied to suggest ways of fixing the system flaws that led to them.

We have found also that in developing and using their own checklists, people are greatly helped by things we have learned from their predecessors. Hence the purpose of this chapter is to provide further background information that will help to assure successful use of Personal Quality Checklists. We briefly introduced these issues in Chapter 2, including especially problems of discouragement when external circumstances make adherence to standards more difficult. In this chapter we shall provide greater depth and many examples.

1. PROBLEMS IN IMPLEMENTATING CHECKLISTS

Several problems may arise in the development of the initial checklist:

° Failure to provide an operational definition of each defect standard, thus making it difficult to recognize when a defect occurs or leading to inconsistency in recording defects. One particularly frustrating problem arises when your own performance cannot be easily separated from that of the systems on which you depend. Suppose you find, for example, that someone has not received the letter you wrote two weeks ago. It is possible that you misaddressed the letter or forgot to mail it. It is also possible that there was failure at any one of the subsequent steps in the delivery process: your company mailroom, the U.S. Postal Service, the recipient's mailroom, or the recipient herself. The letter may be forever lost, or it may turn up later at any one of a number of locations. This example brings out clearly that personal quality is not the whole story: our personal quality depends in part on the systems within which we work.

° A list that has too few waste-reducers and time-savers by comparison with additional activity-expanding activities. One needs to save time to make room for new activities. Otherwise only frustration will result. We have suggested that if you must err, err on the side of too many waste-reducers.

° Inclusion of standards that in themselves require major, special attention. Overweight and lack of fitness are two common examples. If one's weight is already satisfactory, for example, a standard like Sergesketter's "Weight below 190 pounds" will suffice; but if one is seriously overweight, a good program for weight reduction and fitness may be needed. However, even for the overweight, it can be helpful to include a single checklist standard like "Snacking between meals" that may address an important cause of the problem. The quality principle involved here is that good results are obtained only by working on the underlying processes that lead to the results. (As we have said, an attempt to achieve results without dealing with processes is like keeping your eye on the scoreboard rather than the ball.)

° Some standards may accumulate so many defects that one may spend excessive time in recording them. An example might be, "Failure to recover promptly from interruptions." This might be temporarily removed from the list while the system was redesigned or reengineered to reduce interruptions to a rate that could be coped with.

° Some people want to record not only defects but opportunities for defects. In principle, this permits more satisfactory statistical analysis. In practice, it is likely to be data-gathering overkill. In some cases it is literally impossible: for example, we have pointed out that all individual opportunities for accidents cannot be easily enumerated.

° As we mentioned at the end of Chapter 2, defects may rise because of increased job demands that create more opportunities for defects. This can be discouraging. Since counting opportunities for defects is usually too time-consuming, the checklist user may get indirect measures of job intensity. For example, for someone working mainly on invoicing, the total number of invoices processed might be a good measure of job intensity. Then the number of defects might be divided by the number of invoices to obtain an index that makes some allowance for job intensity. If the checklist user knew something about statistical regression analysis, the number of invoices could be used as an independent variable in a regression for which defects are the dependent variable.

° A few have felt that emphasis on "defects" is a negative approach. There are two good answers: (1) it's usually easier to keep track of defects than the things done right; (2) only defects point the way to improvement of the underlying processes.

° However, for those who want to count successes, the checklist idea will work just as well. Or, in a list mainly devoted to counting defects, some standards for which successes are counted can be added and tabulated separately. For fitness, for example, you can keep track of the number of hours of exercise or some measure of output, such as miles walked or jogged, holes of golf, sets of tennis, or laps of swimming. Other possible examples: number of conversations with direct reports (for a manager), calls on potential new customers (for a salesman), quality improvement projects worked on (for anyone). Further discussion of this approach is provided in the next section.

° One friend, who is very well organized to begin with, rejected the idea of a checklist because he felt that it would provoke unnecessary anxiety. Another friend, who is very badly organized to begin with, rejected the idea of a checklist because he thought it would be too hard to implement.

2. EXPLOITING GENERAL TQM TOOLS

Personal Quality Checklists often lead to insightful analyses that draw on a wide range of TQM ideas and tools. Elementary improvement tools like flowcharts, cause-and-effect diagrams, and Pareto analysis can be applied to one's own activities. (Some of these tools will be illustrated in later chapters.) When checklists are used in TQM training courses, the presentation of each TQM tool can be followed up with a required exercise in application of the tool to some personal activity, usually helping to improve on a difficult standard on the checklist. Since TQM tools are best learned by applying them as soon as possible after initial instruction, personal quality provides an indispensable support to any form of TQM training.

As checklist data are accumulated, tools of statistical process control, intervention analysis, and experimental design can be applied. Just-In-Time principles can be invoked; for example, William Ragland, a student at the University of Chicago, designed a Kanban scheme for his in-basket:

DESK KANBAN OVERFLOW

The goal of never more than one project on the desk at a time did not prove to be workable. . . . I have adopted a modified Kanban. The nature of [my] engineering work often involves extended projects and reports. I took a standard five-bin vertical file and modified it to make three larger and sloped-sided bins. Using the five bins seemed too much temptation for it to become a storage container. Each of the three bins has either a red, yellow, or green colored tab to identify it. . . . The colors indicate an approximate priority to each task (another reason to keep it to three bins). The system I use is that material is removed from only one bin at a time for use on the desk. If someone brings temporary material, e.g., for immediate discussion, I can scoop up the stuff on the desk and put it in the empty bin and then rapidly retrieve it later. The additional bins serve as hold for projects that are in suspension; for example, documents in typing or projects waiting for other input.

The system has been in operation only for a week, but there have been two positive aspects in addition to having a clean desk. The first is that the action of clearing the material when a colleague brings temporary material for discussion signals complete attention to his or her problem. If additional work is required, I can either file it and list it on a priority list or replace one of the Kanban bins if it is urgent. A second advantage is that when the boss has a hot item, I can identify my three top priority tasks and inquire if he wants one bumped out of the Kanban and which one. This serves to identify his true level of urgency. Otherwise, I determine the priority.

Finally, for teaching of statistical methodology, the checklists provide personal data very quickly that permit practice in simple time-series analysis: fitting of the data leads to exploration of the effects of trend, day-of-week, lags, extraneous variables, and deliberate interventions. In most cases, the trend component is significantly downward within just a few weeks; often, indeed, the improvement is obvious by visual analysis of the time-series plot alone, as it was in the data on Sergesketter displayed in Chapter 1.

An extended example of analysis of actual checklist data is given in the Appendix.

3. VARIATIONS AND EXTENSIONS OF THE PERSONAL QUALITY CHECKLIST

There are variations of the Personal Quality Checklist that retain much of its simplicity. At AT&T, for example, some people have tried to list *missed opportunities:* "an error, a defect, a mismatch, between the product/service and its specification or applicable standard; any mistake that results in customer dissatisfaction." Before he introduced Personal Quality Checklists in his MBA classes, Roberts often encouraged his students to do personal projects in which they measured time spent in desirable activities rather than counting defects—for example, time spent with customers, time spent in training subordinates, or time spent in job-related study or training.

We have explained that two keys to quality improvement are the reduction of defects and the reduction of cycle time. Keeping track of your time is usually harder and more diverting from your normal activities than is counting defects. The same is true of measuring your cycle times for specific processes. However, the extra burden of data collection is sometimes worthwhile. Usually, *such efforts should be regarded as projects distinct from the basic Personal Quality Checklist*, even though the data may be recorded for convenience on the checklist form.

A very simple example of such a project entailed speeding up the time it takes to shave. Roberts found that total shaving time from first initial lathering to final rinsing was consistently close to six minutes. The shaving process entailed two lathering steps, then careful, short, repeated strokes, progressing systematically over the entire skin area, then rinse. Simply trying to shave faster did not help much, so a different approach was taken: One initial lather-rinse stage was eliminated; instead, the first lathering was followed by preliminary shaving with long smooth strokes that quickly covered the entire skin surface; then rinse; touch-up shaving of difficult spots; and final rinse. The total time for this modified shaving process was consistently close to three minutes; shaving time had been cut in half. The whole trial took less than two weeks, and it was entirely separate from the checklist effort. Had Roberts known this result 50 years sooner, he could have saved 900 hours!

Personal fitness provides many illustrations of special improvement projects, separate from the main checklist of defect standards. For example, a typical fitness goal on a checklist might be, "Work out for at least 60 minutes, at least three times a week." Suppose that on a particular day you have only 30 minutes available. The temptation is strong to skip the workout since you will still incur a defect if, say, you work out for 30 minutes. An alternative is to keep a separate record of time spent in working out each day, perhaps using your checklist form to do so. This entails a still modest recording burden. Plotting the data through time on a run chart (time spent is shown on the vertical axis, the days are shown on the horizontal axis) provides reinforcement if the level is high, especially if the trend is upward. Recording and tracking time per day or per week provides strong motivation. (Fortunately, a surprisingly little time spent in exercise will go a surprisingly long way in achieving physical fitness.) The same principle applies to all activity-expanders.

An alternative route to improvement in fitness is to modify the initial standards themselves when it is apparent that they are very difficult to achieve. For example, one checklist user set a standard: "three one-hour workouts a week on the exercise machines at my health club." When she recorded repeated defects, she realized that getting to the health club for a workout took nearly an hour of driving, round trip. By purchasing an exercise machine for use in her own apartment, she was able to complete the entire workout during the time it had taken her to drive to the health club. Defects went down sharply. Again, we have an illustration of Kelling's dictum that improvement is often best achieved by doing things differently.

Weight reduction is another good illustration. Here you can record weights daily, at the same time each day. You may also find it useful to record total calories consumed per day and some measure of exercise.

If you undertake a project like improving personal fitness or losing weight, you should carefully plan in advance how you are going to approach the project. A well-designed program for fitness and/or weight reduction is essential. Our experience with MBA students suggests that general good intentions rarely lead to success.

Studies entailing quantitative measurements will be discussed further in Chapter 4.

More on Defect Counts Versus Measurements

The Personal Quality Checklist is a simpler approach than studies that attempt to measure quantitative variables, such as time spent in working out. Indeed, the checklist is so simple, both in concept and implementation, that Roberts did not think of it for many years when he was supervising personal improvement projects by students in his MBA statistics courses. Nor did he think of making the personal projects done by these students into tools for behavioral modification; he was aiming mainly at getting data that would provide practice in statistical tools, a desirable aim for teaching but not necessarily the best route to improvement. However, it turned out that many of these earlier personal projects did lead to improvement. One example is a study of golf putting, summarized at the start of Chapter 4.

From a statistical perspective, a totally successful Personal Quality Checklist with no defects whatever would be totally uninteresting statistically: just a string of zeros. But it could represent enormous improvement over the prechecklist base performance. So far, only a few people have been this successful, and the data from studies of defects on Personal Quality Checklists have provided useful exercises in statistical analysis, although in most instances the improvement has been pretty obvious from the time-series plot of daily (or weekly or monthly) defects, as was true in Sergesketter's original example.

4. EXPERIENCES WITH PERSONAL QUALITY CHECKLISTS

In teaching TQM, there is no substitute for lots of examples. The general principles in isolation do not hold students' attention or motivate them to apply what they are being exposed to. In this section, we provide more examples. If you think that you already have enough background to go ahead with your own checklist, you can skip them, but we think that most readers will find them helpful.

In the last two years, we have received reports from many people who have tried Personal Quality Checklists and found them useful, often in surprising ways. For example, Beth McDermott, an AT&T sales vice president, introduced the Personal Quality Checklist to the au pair who helps her take care of her twin boys. It has served as a very helpful aid on organizing and aligning all of the activities that are required to get that job done well.

Below we give systematic reports from four students in the Executive Program of the Graduate School of Business, University of Chicago, all from early 1992.

VICE-PRESIDENT/CORPORATE DEVELOPMENT

A noteworthy observation about my project on the Personal Quality Checklist is the amount of attention the project received from other senior managers in my company. Our company has been implementing the quality process for almost three years with varying degrees of success in various work groups. The biggest problem has been to get individual employees to take ownership in their areas of responsibility. The Personal Quality Checklist is a positive way to get each employee involved in improving personal quality on and off the job. I envisage its use in many company work groups in the future.

The project has also benefited me personally by forcing me to focus on several areas of weakness on and off the job and to take action to correct the problems. My checklist:

1. Allocate 30 minutes each day to read technical journals and newsletters.
2. File all reading materials immediately.
3. Spend 10–15 minutes each day talking to subordinates about project status.
4. Work out three times per week for at least 20 minutes.
5. Spend no more than four hours per week on hobby
6. Spend 10–15 minutes each day learning WordPerfect.
7. Update daily personal travel activities into one trip to avoid waste.

My conclusions:

1. In seven weeks I have learned the basics of WordPerfect without taking a training class. I can now prepare simple reports and understand all the basic functions of the program. I still have a lot to learn.
2. After several years without a regular exercise routine, I am now working out at least two times per week and will get to three times per week soon. I feel much better now than I have in several years.
3. I am communicating with my staff better, and we are all more in-

formed on work project issues. I check E-mail regularly and my calendar is always up to date. I am more aware of what is happening in the rest of the company, and I am more organized with respect to overall time management.

4. My statistical analysis showed that there was progressive improvement. The analysis helped me to learn a great deal about basic statistical analysis and how to check my results to be sure that they were statistically sound.

5. The most prominent defect category is failure to read technical journals and newsletters.

VICE-PRESIDENT/AUDITING

Previously, in seeking continuous improvement in my own performance, I was focused on training, education (MBA), presentation skills, staying current on issues, etc. What I've learned is that by focusing on more mundane issues (defect checklist) I have achieved improved performance quickly and have made a substantial impact on my day-to-day performance. My checklist:

1. *Act on first reading of PROFS (electronic mail):* Failure to respond, file, follow-up, delete, delegate, or prioritize an electronic mail message the *first time* it is opened.

2. *Delegate properly—using five-step approach:*

    1. Discuss issue/problem/opportunity.
    2. Decide on exactly what is needed.
    3. Determine the commitment made—*what* will be delivered.
    4. Determine the next follow-up date—*when* will it be delivered.
    5. Set an interim update meeting, if appropriate.

3. *Act on first reading or skimming of written materials:* Failure to respond, file, set follow-up, discard, delegate, or prioritize incoming written material.

4. *Not finishing tasks:* I tend to jump from one project to the next without taking the first project to a natural completion point.

5. *Failure to properly file information for easy access:* Usually results in hunting for things that are missing.

6. *Personal appearance checkpoints:* Full length mirror view before leaving for work, once in the AM, and once in the PM.

7. *Each time I eat anything not on my diet, I will count that as a defect.*

8. *Exercise at least three times a week.*

Specifically, I have found:

- By reading my E-mail and written materials the *first* time and by properly filing my information (to avoid a hunt), I have saved time.
- I have finished more tasks by prioritizing, focusing, doing, and stopping at natural breaks. I have a better sense of accomplishment and I am not duplicating efforts (e.g., reading material twice to get "reacquainted" with where I left off).
- My secretary and I have developed a filing system and a filing note. This eliminated my writing where I want information filed each time and also reminds me of the filing system in place. (Ends up easier to find things.)
- Delegating properly has proven to be a *major driver* in my checklist. By concentrating on the five-step approach, I have saved unnecessary follow-up work, reduced disruptions in my staff's workday, avoided miscommunications with my staff, and lowered my anxiety level. I know when an item is due and what the deliverable is.
- As I suspected, my checklist has shown that I do not place a high priority on my "personal" areas. I don't usually take the time to check my appearance (that is, I get dressed and rush out). I have not made substantial progress in dieting and I did not tackle the exercise defect until I restated the defect. My exercise defects now count when I pass up any opportunity to exercise such as taking the stairs or parking farther from the door.

MANAGER/RESEARCH AND DEVELOPMENT

(This discussion brings out the important point that improvement of personal quality can have positive effects on the productivity of others, quite apart from the saving of one's personal time.)

The first step was to look at the process I work in. I manage a 30-person research and development unit. Success in the development of our products requires clear and timely communication within my group and with other groups and departments in the company. To improve my personal quality I decided to focus on two broad categories of activity—waste and value adding—as they relate to communications. I have also found that I am more effective at work if I exercise regularly, so I decided to improve the consistency of my exercise program too.

The approach was to identify specific defects leading to waste in the way I perform my job, or missed opportunities to perform a value-adding opportunity. To reduce waste in communication, I focused on formal interpersonal communication taking place through planned meetings, and the communications I receive at my desk. The latter fall into three main categories: telephone calls, E-mail, and physical mail. I further subdivided the physical mail into two additional categories: routine "junk" and important items requiring significant time to process. My goal was to reduce the amount of time I wasted by being late to meetings or failing to handle any correspondence I might receive. I realized that by being late to meetings or slow in handling of correspondence, I was not only affecting my own productivity but also the productivity of people who were waiting for me.

I hoped that by reducing waste in these activities, I would have more time available for important value-adding activities that I had too often neglected. I had for years felt that it was important to include "management by wandering around" in my daily routine, and had apparently been slipping. For some time my staff had pointed out to me that I did not spend as much time as I used to talking to them about their ideas, projects, and problems. To better serve these internal customers, I decided to set a goal of meeting informally with each of my staff at least once per week. I also resolved to exercise more frequently.

My checklist:

WASTE ELIMINATION

Late for meeting or appointment: Applies to any meeting, no matter what the cause, and even if others are late. It is always tempting to read one more piece of mail, make a call, or answer an E-mail message. This causes others to be late because I am. One defect per occurrence.

Failure to return phone call within one day: This means within one working day of receipt of the message, either hand delivered or by voice mail. When out of the office I will call in daily for messages. By not returning phone calls promptly, I may be delaying others in completing tasks or missing an important piece of information they were trying to convey to me. One defect per occurrence.

Failure to answer all E-Mail within one day: This means within one working day of receipt of the message, and will apply even if I am away from the office. I will make sure that I give people advance notice of when I will be away, and delegate routine activities so that my absence does not hold up the work of others. Often people send me E-mail messages because they need a decision or direction from me. By failure to respond, I may be delaying an important project. One defect per occurrence.

Handled routine or junk mail more than once: This includes anything that I would take action on immediately or discard following a minute or less of review. Multiple handling of documents is a real time waster, and leads to clutter on my desk, making it difficult to find things. One defect per occurrence.

Handled important mail item more than twice: Important mail requiring careful review or considerable action on my part may be prioritized and placed in a "to do" stack. The next time I handle an item, I should complete any required action. Multiple handling is a sign of putting things off that should be done. This also leads to the cluttered desk problem. One defect per occurrence.

FAILURE TO PERFORM DESIRED ACTIVITIES

Failure to spend time with at least six different employees daily: This means taking the time each week to personally see each of the 30 employees in the R&D group, to ask them about their projects and any problems or ideas they may have. Being an R&D manager is like being a coach. People need to know that I am interested in their progress or projects and ideas. I must be available to help resolve problems that they cannot resolve. It's easy for me to get caught up in administrative details and forget the coaching aspect of my job. My goal is to talk to at least six different people each day of the week. I will "carry forward" to the next day any excess over six, but cannot make up for days when I talked to less than six. This forces me to plan ahead when I will be out of the office, and encourages me to see people before I go away. One defect per employee fewer than six not contacted daily.

Missed one of four planned workouts during the work week: This can be satisfied by weight lifting, running, biking or roller blading, but must be at least 20 minutes of activity to count. I find that I am much more productive all week if I make the time to exercise. Each day I will plan my workout schedule. One defect for each planned workout missed.

Our company is just now beginning its TQM process. There has been much training and team formation, but little action at the individual level as yet. Many employees are asking "when is the quality going to start." I had hoped to identify a simple tool that professionals could use to track their personal quality. The Personal Defect List provided what I was looking for. At the beginning of each week I would enter the previous week's data into an Excel spreadsheet and post it, along with a run chart, outside my office. People are starting to realize that I am committed to quality improvement and some have begun to keep their own checklists.

The mere act of creating the checklist resulted in immediate improvement in at least two of the categories. Since beginning the project, I have missed only one planned workout and failed to return calls within one business day only twice. During the first five weeks my average number of defects has dropped from over ten to less than two. During this time, my desk has gradually become tidy as I reduced the backlog of accumulated work, and I have actually spent less time at my desk. The elimination of waste and recycle has allowed me to spend more time on previously neglected but important activities.

ACCOUNTING MANAGER

The objective of my personal defect tracking was to eliminate/reduce mindless time caused by:

- ° Sifting through a piled-up in-box, of either company mail or junk mail, at various times throughout the week.
- ° Forgetting to do little tasks that were needlessly put on hold.
- ° Feeling flustered due to a buildup of little tasks that were needlessly put on hold.
- ° Feeling inadequate since I had not kept up on current events.
- ° Searching through home or office files for documents that had not been filed yet.
- ° Searching for inadequately organized PC files.
- ° Recreating accidentally erased PC files, which were not properly backed up.
- ° Re-questioning people, since I had not listened properly the first time through a conversation—so I had to go back and ask the proper questions I should have asked the first time.

Tracking defects has helped me to get *organized* and I truly believe I get more accomplished *every day!* Since I am not generally a disorganized person, the habits above tend to fluster me, because they cause disorganization. Although I still have defects, I find that just paying attention to defects has helped me to:

- ° Stay abreast of company and world current events (although I still have periods of putting off reading the newspaper).
- ° Feel less flustered since I have:
  A *clean* in-box,
  Organized files both at home and at the office,
  Fewer little tasks on hold,
  Not lost or looked for one disorganized PC file in seven weeks,
  And not looked for many lost items over the past seven weeks.

° Listen to people—and I think that they are noticing. Less and less I find I need to re-question prior discussions.
° Be more pleasant—and since I am less disorganized, have more time and accomplish more, I find myself generally in better moods than before.

My checklist:

Read newspaper at least five times/weekly: Everyone should be continually aware of current events. In my job, I should always be up to date on world, national, and local news, especially financial news and foreign exchange markets. Somehow I manage to shirk this very important activity, with excuses of too much else to do—which are unacceptable—and then spend inefficient time trying to catch up on what is happening in the news. Lack of current news knowledge can also affect the quality of my work.

Read company and other professional news promptly: This is an activity any professional needs to do. Not being continually current regarding news of your own company and profession is unacceptable. Too often these items clutter my in-basket at work or my magazine rack at home, and either get read too late or not at all. Same excuses/problems as above.

Search for something lost or misplaced: More than momentary confusion as to location of important document, book, address, working materials, keys, etc. Forgetting a task or working material is included here.

Putting a small task in a hold file: My work-in-process files, both at office and at home, must be kept small and attacked continually. Note: two important "small tasks" include filing and informing someone of unpleasant news.

Failure to discard incoming junk promptly: Although I am getting better at this, I still need improvement in skimming incoming mail and other reading materials for unnecessary clutter and immediate discarding. Hold-in-case is cleaned out at least once a week.

Failure to regularly organize and back up PC files: PC files should be properly labeled and menued as they are originated and backed up daily. Too often I cannot recognize/remember file names and need to search for needed files, due to inadequate labeling/filing. Additionally, proper menuing avoids the necessity of sifting through all PC files to properly menu. Because of the nomad nature of my current job function, there is no access to network/automated back-up, so I need to back up manually on a daily basis.

Study for classes in executive MBA program on average three hours/daily: Organized and effective learning will be realized only with continual progress on school work through good study habits. This will avoid crunch "all-nighters," short-term memory learning, and inefficient/low-quality assignment completion due to lack of learning course content.

Failure to listen carefully and question fully: At times my mind does wander. When I do listen, I generally ask all pertinent questions, but when my mind wanders I lack the ability to ask needed questions. Be continually alert to communications and question appropriately, to avoid wasteful hours of backtracking for needed information.

Unpleasantness: I get too caught up in what I am doing and too often show irritation or frustration. This is a very important issue: Many times I am too outwardly obvious about these feelings.

4

OTHER ROUTES TO PERSONAL QUALITY IMPROVEMENT

1. ROUTES BASED ON DETAILED MEASUREMENTS RATHER THAN PERSONAL QUALITY CHECKLISTS

Personal Quality Checklists are simple and powerful tools for the enhancement of personal quality, but they are far from the only tools. In this chapter we consider other approaches that can supplement or extend checklists.

As explained in Chapter 3, for many years before Sergesketter's experimentation with Personal Quality Checklists at AT&T, Roberts permitted MBA students in statistics and Total Quality Management courses to do personal projects if they did not have convenient access to organizations and organizational data. Over the years there were many good personal projects, and most of these were aimed at personal improvement.

These projects included improvement of foreign language skills or of free-throw shooting, getting a fast start in the morning or losing weight, improving fitness or coping with medical problems like hypertension or multiple sclerosis, and finding the quickest commutation routes. One couple even improved their ability to get their young child to bed at the desired time.

These studies were all personal applications of TQM ideas. All entailed measurement of performance, and most involved deliberate attempts to intervene to improve performance, with careful statistical analysis to see if the intervention had been successful. Most of these studies were based on quantitative data rather than tallying of individual defects.

By comparison with Personal Quality Checklists, these earlier personal improvement projects typically required relatively elaborate design, data collection, and analysis. Weight-loss attempts, for example, entailed daily measurements of weight, caloric intakes, caloric outgo in exercise, and auxiliary information as well. Many of the projects were substantial successes, and virtually all students got valuable experience with relatively sophisticated data analysis.

Example: Improvement of Putting

One student's objective was to improve his putting:

An essential step in improvement is checking whether an apparent improvement is genuine. This is the "check" stage of the Shewhart/Deming PDCA cycle (plan-do-check-act). (In practice, people often want to take the easy way out and bypass the "check" stage, but this is hazardous.)

The stage prior to "check"—that is, the "do" stage—was an attempt to improve a personal process by a student in an MBA course in TQM. The student, an excellent golfer who had never been satisfied with his putting, set up an indoor putting green for careful practice and experimentation. Results of the first 2000 putts of his study, summarized by groups of 20 each, are shown below:

Putts sunk per 100 trials from fixed distance.

47	57	57	52	59	64	45	58	61	57
71	61	67	59	64	66	76	58	61	65

At the end of the first 10 groups of 100, he noticed that 136 of 443 misses were left misses and 307 were right misses. He reasoned that the position of the ball relative to the putting stance was a problem. "I concluded that the ball was too far 'back' (too much in the middle) of my putting stance. I moved the ball several inches forward in my stance, keeping it just inside my left toe." The final 10 observations were made with the modified stance.

Note the significance of the previous two steps: He thought to keep auxiliary data on right versus left misses. He noticed the surprising pattern in these right and left misses and formulated a shrewd hypotheses as to a process change that might lead to improvement: He changed his stance. This is very much in the spirit of TQM: learning from experience how to do things differently and, it is hoped, better.

To show what was going on, Figure 2 displays the data in a run chart of the percentage of successful putts in 20 successive groups of 100 putts each. For ease of visual interpretation, we have connected successive points. Visual examination of the plot, the first step, suggests that the student is improving: On average, the last ten points are higher than the first ten.

We'd like to decide whether this improvement is or is not a chance fluke. Statistical analysis—not shown here—suggests that the improvement is genuine. A more subtle question is whether we're seeing the steady improvement that comes with practice, a sharp improvement due to the change in stance, or both combined.

Further statistical analysis—not shown here—suggests that the change of stance is responsible for the improvement. Moreover, the improvement is substantial, an estimated 16 percent. It amounts to several strokes per round.

This illustration is a simple example of what has been labeled "intervention analysis" by George Box and George Tiao in a classic paper, "Intervention Analysis with Applications to Economic and Environmental Problems," in the *Journal of the American Statistical Association*, 1975, Vol. 70, pp. 70–79. Of all the more "advanced" statistical tools, intervention

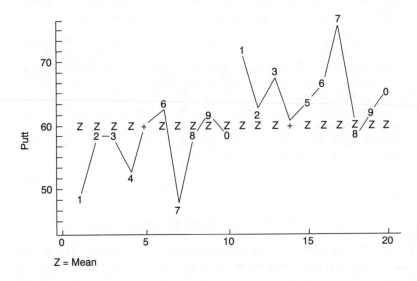

Figure 2

analysis is probably the most important, since it can be used almost every time the PDCA cycle is implemented.

There are no randomized controls, as in "true" statistical experimentation. But, if you take care in interpretation, conclusions from intervention analysis rest on nearly as firm ground. When randomized controls are possible, statistical analysis can be even more conclusive. But in many attempts to improve processes, especially service processes, randomized controls are not feasible and we must rely on intervention analysis.

The Interocular Traumatic Test (ITT)

In the putting example, simple visual analysis of the run chart makes it apparent that the improvement in performance is genuine. The only real need for statistical analysis is to shed light on whether we are seeing a gradual improvement due to practice, or an abrupt improvement due to the change of technique.

The most important statistical lesson is to plot the data and see if the conclusion is apparent by simple visual analysis alone. To make this point vivid, Joseph Berkson, an M.D. with a Ph.D. in statistics, who worked for many years at the Mayo Clinic, coined the humorous but highly suggestive expression, *Interocular Traumatic Test (ITT)*: "The message of the data should hit you between the eyes."

In TQM we always aim to get such substantial improvements that the ITT will be conclusive. No need then to fool around with fancy statistics! However, there are often applications in which there is a great deal of noise in the quality data: There are big variations from one period to the next even in the absence of any identifiable causes. In such applications, the effects of an intervention that is in fact a substantial improvement may not be easy to disentangle from the background noise. It is for these applications that we need the statistical tools of intervention analysis.

Limitations of the Early Student Personal Projects

In these early projects in Roberts's classes, there was relatively little success on the improvement of work processes, which, for full-time students, translates into improvement of studying efficiency. Elaborate logging or work sampling (see Section 14) to find out how students were spending time sometimes helped. One student found that he spent over 20 hours a week watching television, much more than he had realized; others found that they spent a lot of time woolgathering when they thought they were studying. But breakthroughs were rare. Roberts tried to get students to log obvious mistakes and errors—for example, losing things and having to spend time in search—with the aim of learning how to prevent these recurrences. Students were reluctant to try this. Also, Roberts did not try to improve his own work performance along the lines that he was exhorting students to follow in order to improve their study efficiency.

Sergesketter's Personal Quality Checklist was the answer to these disappointments. It also led to the use of other quality tools for improvement of personal quality. These tools, and examples of their use, are given in the balance of this chapter.

2. USE OF OTHER QUALITY IMPROVEMENT TOOLS

Personal Quality Checklist studies or studies based on quantitative measures like the putting example can be supplemented by other quality improvement tools, such as those presented in a useful quality booklet, *The Memory Jogger*,™ by GOAL/QPC that are presented in almost all TQM training courses.

Consider studies to improve fitness. You may keep track of reasons for missing workouts and do a Pareto analysis to find which reasons seem most important. Essentially this entails tabulating the number of times each reason occurs and then focusing improvement efforts on the reasons that occur most frequently. (A simple example of Pareto analysis is given in the Appendix.)

Or you can do a cause-and-effect diagram of possible root causes of missing workouts. This is essentially a listing of major categories of root causes, with a listing of individual root causes within each major category.

With the insight thus gained, you can then try to design a fitness program that is consistent both with your psychology (most people can find *some* fitness activity that they enjoy) and with your circumstances (one student obtained substantially improved fitness simply by substituting stair climbing for the use of the elevator whenever it was practicable for her to do so).

Similar observations apply to studies aimed at control of obesity, except that for this purpose the simple Personal Quality Checklist may sometimes be superior to elaborate record keeping with calorie counting and weight measurement. For example, some have made major progress in weight control by simply dealing with one aspect of the overall problem with a standard on the checklist. For example:

° No snacking after 7 P.M.
° Eliminating sugar and cream from coffee
° Substitution of low-fat for high-fat foods
° Cutting chocolate consumption in half

3. ELIMINATION OF CONSTRAINTS

A broad concept can lead to improvement of personal quality (as well as improvement of quality in general): elimination of constraints on activities that serve no useful purpose. If we view a particular task—or physical layout or way of thinking—as necessary to the achievement of the end result we are aiming at, we are in effect accepting that task or layout or way of thinking as a *constraint* on our work processes. A key idea of TQM is to improve quality by eliminating needless constraints. (Recall the example in Chapter 1 of runners walking around a rattlesnake rather than trying to push it off the trail with a branch!)

Personal checklists tend to force our attention to constraints that can be eliminated. An everyday example is the habit of temporarily holding mail-order catalogs from which we do not intend to place an order, rather than immediately discarding them.

A more complicated constraint is illustrated by one student's experience with a personal checklist. She was failing consistently to meet her exercise standard; she was skipping workouts because she felt too pressed for time. Upon reflection, she realized that just getting to and from the gym took substantial time and contributed nothing to fitness. Her workouts emphasized light free weights, and she concluded that a small investment would permit her to do them in her own apartment and eliminate the trips to the gym. (In a similar example, in Chapter 3, an indoor exercising machine filled the role of the exercise machines at the health club.)

Eliminating constraints can also be thought of in terms of elimination of waste, since any constraint that can be eliminated really represents waste. We recognize the waste only when we eliminate the constraint. In the next section, we turn to what is usually called waste elimination.

4. SYSTEMATIC APPROACHES TO THE ELIMINATION OF WASTE

Waste is any process step or procedure that could be eliminated without harm or that could be done more efficiently, that is, faster or cheaper. Waste is a relative concept: whenever we discover a process improvement, the old process is seen to be wasteful.

The relentless attack on waste is a central management strategy at leading Japanese companies. Japanese suggestion systems, which generate large numbers of waste-removal improvements, are just one manifestation. The development of Just-In-Time manufacturing at Toyota was essentially a consequence of a search for waste reduction that lasted for about two decades.

Identification of waste is not always easy, even in manufacturing. The most obvious forms of waste are mistakes and blunders, defective product, scrap, rework, and the like. But there are others just as harmful, that are not obvious. You have to observe carefully how you work and ask whether anything you are doing could be speeded up or eliminated. Usually, elimination is the more successful approach. But recognizing waste isn't easy when you haven't thought about it.

Waste Reduction in Report Writing

An executive decided to tackle improvement of her ability to write reports as the object of a personal improvement project. She followed good TQM procedures by flowcharting the process by which she prepared a report, from the assignment and initial planning to the delivery of the completed report. The flowchart showed that much of the activity consisted of delivering a handwritten draft to a typist, typing, proofreading, retyping. The same process was repeated if she revised the first draft to make a second draft.

It occurred to her that substantial waste could be removed if she simply keyed in the first draft herself, using a word processor and a PC. Typing was no problem; she knew how to type, but she had accepted without reflection the constraint (becoming rapidly obsolete) that executives do not do their own typing. Using the word processor, she found that the whole process was much shortened, since the handwriting step was eliminated completely. Moreover, she could type more rapidly than she could write, and she found that her written expression improved because of the ease with which she could make revisions in the process of composition, something much more difficult to do when writing by hand. Also, she could use a spell-checker to catch misspellings and ease proofreading.

(Both authors have used the PC keyboard for composition for many years. Roberts learned to type when a secretary on his first job told him that she couldn't read his writing. He followed a high school typing text for less than an hour a day for three weeks and was able to give the secretary rough-typed first drafts. With the advent of word processing and easy correction of errors, the rough-typing stage was eliminated.)

A similar application entailing process mapping is given late in this chapter.

Types of Waste to Look For

One way to sensitize yourself to waste is to look at listings of types of waste. These were mostly drawn up for manufacturing, but the principles are universal. Several such lists are shown below. There is some, but not complete, duplication among these lists. Seeing them all together may heighten your ability to recognize wasteful activity, including waste in your own personal activities.

Tim Fuller, quality consultant and lecturer at the University of Chicago, has emphasized one particular waste, the waste of rework required when something was not done properly in the first place. He calls this form of waste "complexity" because rework loops superimposed on an ideal process flow chart gives the chart a much more complicated appearance. Fuller distinguishes two major forms of complexity: internal and external. Internal rework arises from errors made within a department, while external rework is imposed on the department from the outside.

Fuller advocates the use of work sampling—observation of what you are doing at randomly chosen times that are signaled, say, by the beeping of a digital countdown watch—to identify rework as opposed to "real work"—and to classify rework as external or internal. It turns out that for many people, "real work" is a surprisingly small percentage of total time. For example, systems programmers may spend most of their time fixing flaws in existing programs; Fuller has not yet found a systems programmer who spends as much as five percent of total time on "real work." Work sampling is potentially a valuable tool for improving personal performance because it sensitizes you to the extent and types of internal complexity you may be creating for yourself.

Here are some of the better-known lists of wastes:

TOYOTA'S SEVEN WASTES (OHNO)

° Waste of overproduction [Also irregular production: the end-of-month or end-of-quarter surge]
° Waste of time on hand (waiting)
° Waste in transportation
° Waste of processing itself
° Waste of stock on hand (inventory)
° Waste of movement
° Waste of making defective products, which leads to Fuller's "complexity"

CANON'S NINE WASTES

° Waste caused by work-in-process
° Waste caused by defects
° Waste in equipment
° Waste in expenses
° Waste in indirect labor
° Waste in planning
° Waste in human resources
° Waste in operations
° Waste in startup

SCHONBERGER'S NONOBVIOUS WASTES

° Promotional waste (negative selling)
° Waste of tracking the orders
° Waste of automating the waste

- Container-to-container waste
- Waste of analyzing the waste
- Waste of costing the cost reductions
- Waste of costing the bad quality
- Waste of reporting the utilization and efficiency

FURTHER WASTES

- A starter: collecting unneeded (or unused) data (it isn't *always* desirable to "get some data")
- Another: unnecessary delay in switching from one task to another
- An inspection is wasteful if the average cost of inspection exceeds the average benefits from inspection. However, when an inspection discovers a defect, there is a benefit because further bad consequences of the defect are prevented. If the average cost of inspection is *less* than the average benefits, inspection is then *not* wasteful. See Section 7 for further discussion.

ADDITIONAL WASTEFUL ACTIVITIES (TIM FULLER)

- Sorting to prioritize
- Repeating work
- Hunting for things that are missing
- Doing tasks that serve no purpose
- Walking and not carrying something when it would be easy to do so

Fuller's waste, "Doing tasks that serve no purpose," is implicit in many of the lists, but Fuller does a great service by bringing it out in the open. There is no quicker way to substantial quality improvement than to eliminate tasks that serve no purpose. Often a process flowchart brings out such tasks. Unnecessary approvals that slow down processes are a common example.

Willard Zangwill's Generalization: Most Work Is Waste

Fuller's studies have shown that complexity (rework), caused by internal or external errors, can account for a big fraction of work time. "Real work" is only a small fraction. Thus enormous improvements would be possible if errors could be eliminated. But even "real work" can include a substantial component of waste, so there would be room for still more improvement even if all errors could be eliminated. For further discussion of Fuller's ideas, see Section 14 of this chapter.

Professor Willard Zangwill of the University of Chicago says that the closer you look, the more waste you see. Elimination of waste makes it easier to see additional waste in the remaining activities. His suggestive conclusion is that most work is waste.

Waste and Removal of Constraints

Sometimes people feel that they are not adding value when their work includes wasteful steps. Rework, for example, is thought of as economically valueless. But given that a product needs rework before the customer can accept it, value in the economic sense is added by the rework. However, if the need for rework had been eliminated in the first place, a cost saving would have been realized. The need for rework, in turn, can be eliminated only if some change is made in the process; that is, if some process constraint is removed.

Hence when we talk of eliminating waste, we are really talking about removing constraints on the process that led to the waste.

Suggested Exercise on Personal Waste

Try observing the things you do over a typical work day. How many wasteful activities can you detect? Is the wasteful activity controllable or uncontrollable? If controllable, can you reduce or eliminate it? (This is one good way to get standards for personal checklists.)

Brainstorming on Wastes

It is useful to be sensitive to wastes of any kind, personal or organizational. In a recent MBA class, students brainstormed about examples of waste. Selected illustrations are given below:

° Doing a detailed statistical analysis when the conclusion is obvious by the ITT.

- Prolonging a team meeting long after agreement is reached because everyone wants to register grounds for concurrence in the decision.
- TQM training months before an opportunity for application will arise.
- Going through all the steps of a quality improvement project when a promising improvement is unearthed at an early step. Go ahead and try it out: intervention analysis! (However, avoid blind trial and error.)
- Asking unnecessary questions on a questionnaire.
- Forming a team to do an improvement project that can be better done by a single individual.
- Doing a field test when the answer cannot affect the decision one way or another.
- Gathering performance data that will never by analyzed.
- "Saving money" by limiting training costs on expensive new equipment.
- Distributing reports that no one reads.
- Taking an extra copy of a handout "just in case".
- Running off more xerox copies than needed, "just in case".
- Keeping a stack of items to work on later; allowing the stack to grow without taking care of it.
- Taking training that you won't have time to implement.
- Working until 10 or 11 P.M. without accomplishing anything meaningful, because of not wanting to go home. Productivity of office workers is often terribly low because of this. (From a Japanese student)
- Picking up and processing student loan checks at three separate locations, with three different people, instead of doing everything at one location with one worker.
- Opening mail, putting it aside, then attending to it later.
- In software development, the same tests of code run by the developer and by Quality Assurance.
- Overanalysis of an investment project when the bottom line is already known: paralysis by sensitivity analysis.
- Collection of data that won't serve any useful purpose.
- Excessive filing of materials that can be retrieved from scratch later if actually needed.
- Not asking a client why we got a deal. Asking why we got a deal is just as valuable as asking why we lost one.
- Many people traveling to meet with a single individual because that individual has the higher rank.

- Collecting damages from a contractor when the amount collected doesn't even cover the time spent calculating the amount.
- In one Japanese company, any investment over $833.33 has to be approved by 13 directors and managers when only 3 of the 13 are responsible. The other 10 are just for formality. (From a Japanese student)
- Retaining fliers in campus mail folders after first reading.
- Not compromising quickly enough in fruitless arguments.
- Sticking with an antiquated computer system.
- Being too polite to telemarketers. Just say, "I'm not interested; thanks for calling."
- At bursar's office: six windows to pay bills, only two take credit cards, and these are not marked. People often wait in the wrong line. Manager's response: "We don't want to encourage credit card use, so we don't put signs up for the windows that offer this service."
- Manual entry of authorization code on phone calls. Program code into abbreviated dialing procedure.
- Accounting data on hours billed to specific projects, where the information is provided too late to help in monitoring time spent.
- Checking the mailbox before noon knowing full well that mail distribution is after noon.
- Going through direct-mail coupon books. I've never found one we've used in two years.

5. JUST-IN-TIME AT THE PERSONAL LEVEL

Quite apart from the applications thus far discussed, personal quality can serve as a vehicle for illustrating important TQM principles. We illustrate by a consideration of the issue, "Why the best batch size of a service process may be one."

There are important TQM ideas bearing upon the organization of production processes. These ideas are often grouped under the heading of "Just-In-Time" (JIT). They are easy to visualize in terms of manufacturing. They carry over to service processes, but the carryover is not easy to visualize. We shall now show how you might establish the carryover in terms of *personal processes*. We assume that some of your activities, like ours, are relatively small, frequent, and varied tasks. JIT concepts can help us to cope with them.

Consider an example from educational administration: the processing of requests for reconsideration by rejected MBA applicants in a business school. Replies to these requests were deferred until a substantial pile or batch had accumulated; then, in one sustained effort, replies were prepared and sent out. This is "batch processing," which, according to TQM, is "bad." It's better to answer each request as it comes in; make the batch size one. This is one of the ideas of JIT processing. Is it counterintuitive?

A Simple Personal Example

Many of us can view our work in terms of incoming requests that have to be processed. For example, a student hands in a progress report on a Personal Quality Checklist project. The teacher's task is to write detailed comments and suggestions on the report and return it to the student. It is desirable for the student to receive this feedback as quickly as possible.

The progress reports may be handed in at class, mailed or sent overnight, faxed, given to the teacher's secretary, stuffed under the teacher's office door, sent by E-mail, or hand delivered to the teacher's office or mailbox.

Under batch processing, the teacher could accumulate reports until a convenient time, read them all at once, and return the batch of papers at a subsequent class session. Thus the teacher waits until he or she can switch to "paper reading" mode and apply full concentration to that task.

There are disadvantages to this batch approach:

○ The teacher is accumulating an inventory, in the form of a pile of papers on the desk, which probably leaves less work space for other tasks.
○ Some inventory management may be needed, for example, it may be convenient to alphabetize the papers.
○ As the inventory builds up, the students are not getting feedback. They will be stuck with whatever misunderstanding and confusion they had when they wrote their reports.
○ The teacher is handling each paper twice before processing can begin: it is put into inventory, then taken out to be processed. This is wasteful.

- As the papers are read in batch mode, an inventory of finished goods is built up. This, too, may require some management.
- Only a tiny part of the cycle time for each paper is spent in processing it. The rest is delay or storage.
- Even after a paper has been read and comments recorded, the student will receive these comments only after considerable delay.

Here is an idealized alternative, in the spirit of JIT:

- All students submit their progress reports via fax.
- The teacher reads and comments on each report immediately, and immediately returns it, with comments, by fax.

This alternative has a number of benefits:

- The students receive feedback within, say, an hour or two, rather than after several days.
- Errors or misunderstandings are corrected immediately, thus reducing the time students would have wasted if they had gone ahead, without feedback, to do more work or study.
- The teacher reduces wasted time in having to correct future student misunderstandings. (Misunderstandings tend to harden as they persist.)
- The teacher has no inventory—incoming, in-process, or finished goods—to manage. The desk stays clean. (One aim of JIT is zero inventories, since inventory is seen as intrinsically evil.)
- Paper shuffling is reduced to a minimum.

However, there is also the question of whether individual papers are read more efficiently one at a time or in batch. If paper reading is equally efficient in batch mode and individual mode, the total time spent in actual reading is the same either way. The usual assumption would be that batch mode is more efficient:

1. Only one setup; don't have to keep switching back and forth between different activities.
2. Gain of efficiency by repeatedly doing the same thing.

Just-In-Time principles suggest that these considerations are not necessarily overriding. For one thing, it is possible that task-switching (changeover) costs can be substantially reduced. In manufacturing, for example, it has often been possible to reduce die changes from hours to minutes. In services, little thought has been given to reducing changeover costs, it being assumed that interruptions are very costly and must be avoided whenever possible. It may be, however, that your attitude towards interruptions is the real problem; that if you accept interruptions as inevitable (as is usually in fact true in most service jobs), their effects become less disruptive.

For example, E. C. Olsen, formerly of Geophysical Sciences at the University of Chicago, was able to keep up his research even when he was on administrative assignments. How did he do it? "It's easy. I do my research between phone calls." Olsen was extraordinary, because research typically demands sustained concentration. Most small tasks arising in administration do not require sustained concentration. Rather, they require a tolerance for changing mental focus. It may be that this tolerance can be cultivated.

It may also be true that the assumed efficiency from repetition of the same task is illusory. In reading student progress reports, for example, Roberts has found that the batch mode is *less* efficient. Even for interesting reports on quality improvement projects, reading papers in batch has much the same mind-numbing effects as reading a batch of examinations. Variety in small tasks can be conducive to efficiency!

Other TQM ideas suggest further improvements of the process. For example:

- Smooth out the incoming flow. For example, give students an incentive to submit their papers at any time during the week or term.
- Encourage students to ask questions by telephone, giving them a wide time band in which calls will be welcomed.
- Make it easy for students to find the teacher in his or her office and ask questions without an advance appointment.
- On phone requests for appointments to discuss the projects, see if the questions can be answered immediately over the phone.
- Find faster ways to transmit papers back and forth. E-mail used to be excellent when students made substantial use of it. Faxing is most attractive now.

Extensions of the Example

Suppose now that the teacher has two somewhat different classes, but that each requires projects and progress reports. The temptation to process in batch would be even stronger, since any merging of the two streams of progress reports into a single heterogeneous stream sounds very difficult.

Again, the decision between batch and JIT turns on changeover costs and efficiency from repetition. Confronted by this challenge recently when he had two classes during the same term, Roberts opted for the JIT approach, and it worked as well as it had for a single class.

Another interesting extension of the example would be to complicate the teacher's evaluation task: suppose that there are really two distinct phases of the evaluation—evaluation of the written exposition and checking out on the computer work—and that the latter requires hands-on access to a computer. It might be reasoned that these two activities pose such different requirements that they should be uncoupled—done separately—possibly in separate locations.

For example, if the computer were substantially removed from the teacher's desk, the reading chore might be completed for a batch of papers at the desk, then the batch of papers moved (possibly after temporary storage in inventory) to the computer for the computer checking. In this extension, batching and decoupling turn out to be wasteful; it's better to run the reports one at a time through both steps of the process, even arranging to have a computer at the location at which the evaluation of the written exposition is accomplished.

By considering these possibilities at the personal level, we begin to see more general principles about quality for any process, manufacturing or service. The basic idea is to push tasks through the process without delay, rather than wait to build up batches to be processed at a later time. In setting up processes, we should aim for uninterrupted flow through the process. A key to being able to do this is minimal changeover time from one operation to another or one task to another. Another key is to avoid errors in any stage of the process. But if errors do occur, they are much harder to detect and correct in batch mode; moreover, they are more costly and prevention of recurrence is more difficult.

When we go beyond the personal level to consider processes in which many people participate, the tasks are more complicated, but the ideas developed at the personal level may supply some useful insights.

Extension to All Relatively Routine, Small Tasks

The reasoning applies to small tasks other than student progress reports. That's why Roberts's personal quality checklist has the standard, "Putting a small task in a 'hold pile.'" Another helpful standard is: "Failure to discard incoming junk promptly. (In case of doubt, you can set up a contingency hold file, which is frequently and quickly reviewed and largely purged.)

For incoming reading materials, quick browsing is needed to see whether or not any item should be treated as junk. Try not to set aside "to be read when time is available." At least, do a quick screening to see if you are really likely to want to spend more time on the item later.

Just-In-Time processing is a good aim even if you can't quite do it literally. Keep the batch size as small as possible even if you can't always keep it at one.

Small Tasks

It is sometimes urged that small tasks be prioritized: sort through them and decide which is most important, so that you can do the most important things first. This temptation should be resisted unless a crisis deadline looms! Prioritizing entails added time and paper handling; it does not add value.

Big Tasks

Mixed in with the inflow of small tasks are the big tasks, ones that could take a whole day or more or that must necessarily be accomplished over a longer time period. For a university teacher, these big tasks include such items as:

- Research projects
- Substantial writing (e.g., referee's reports)
- Teaching preparation
- Writing textbooks or monographs
- Speeches

You must prioritize, organize, schedule, and tolerate an inventory of the big tasks.

How do the big tasks get done if you attempt Just-In-Time processing for small tasks? Will efficiency and promptness in processing small tasks lead to slippage on the big ones? Only if you are doing "unnecessary" small tasks, or at least small tasks that you cannot keep pace with, given present resources, no matter how much you improve efficiency.

One test: How many small tasks currently "fall between the cracks"? Although TQM suggests adding total resources only as a last resort, there are times when this alternative deserves consideration! Otherwise, you may become "trapped" by your job!

On balance, so long as you are not doing unnecessary small tasks, greater efficiency with small tasks makes more time for dealing with the large tasks!

Managing the Big Tasks (the Services Job Shop)

One approach is to manage the big tasks by checklists and periodic performance reviews. You should organize the inventory of such tasks so that you can get started on any one of them with minimum loss of time. If you are falling behind generally, you must review *both* the big and the small tasks.

- You may decide that you are spending too much time on small information requests from people who are only very indirectly "customers" of your organization.
- Some major tasks are "good things" in principle, but are not of really high priority in the light of everything else.
- You may even need more help or a bigger budget (but resist the temptation to jump to that conclusion too quickly)!

Small Batch Size: A Numerical Example

ORIGINAL PROCEDURE

- Class of 80 students. Paper to be handed in only at once-weekly class meetings.
- Twelve minutes to read and comment on each paper (five papers per hour).

° Set aside two eight-hour days for batch processing.
° During those 16 hours, each paper is being processed only 12 minutes. Response ratio—total cycle time divided by actual processing time—is 16 hours/12 minutes = 80/1.
° Papers returned next class: overall cycle time, seven days.
° Suppose that students don't procrastinate but finish their papers during the week before they are due, uniformly in time.
° Overall cycle time is 3.5 + 7.0 = 10.5 days.

ALTERNATIVE PLAN

° As soon as students finish their papers, they fax them to the teacher.
° As soon as the teacher receives their papers, he or she reads, comments on, and returns them by fax.
° Overall cycle time is now measured in minutes or hours, not days. The response ratio is sharply reduced.
° Students benefit from fast response—errors corrected promptly, no more lost time because of them.
° No inventory of unread papers at any stage of the process—receiving, work-in-process, or finished goods. The teacher's desk stays uncluttered.

6. IMPROVING PERSONAL QUALITY BY BENCHMARKING

Bob Galvin has remarked that the idea of benchmarking is to "steal anything that isn't proprietary." Someone has suggested adding: "and improve on it." Benchmarking contrasts with the common tendency to be suspicious of anything that was "not invented here" (which is even given an acronym, NIH). For many organizations, benchmarking is a major contributor to TQM. These organizations may do benchmarking at different levels. For example,

° Benchmarking within one's own organization.
° Industry benchmarking.
° Benchmarking on outstanding organizations: Milliken, Honda, Disney, etc.
° Benchmarking by comparing internal organizational processes

against the corresponding processes in other organizations, whatever the industry or location anywhere in the world.

For example, in the crisis of the early 1980s, Xerox began by benchmarking on Fuji-Xerox, a Deming prize winner, from whom they learned much. They went on to benchmark each process on the best example they could find. For example, as many companies have done, they benchmarked on the warehousing process of L. L. Bean.

This approach requires finding the best process (or at least a process much better than one's own), deciding what to measure about the process and how, and then working on the implementation of best practices in one's own organization. Benchmarking within an industry may entail phone calls, questionnaires, and site visits. Health care organizations have been doing this kind of benchmarking with effectiveness.

The same approach carries over to the personal level, although necessarily the scope of the search for best practices is much more limited. If you are having trouble using your word processor, for example, it may be easier to seek out an experienced co-worker than to struggle with the manual yourself.

You can also learn more about quality in general by informal benchmarking of outstanding organizational processes that you encounter in everyday life. For example, one of the authors did some unplanned benchmarking when he needed quick, near-emergency medical care on five recent occasions (shingles, cracked ribs, head wound, acute urinary infection, sinusitis). A nearby clinic—Suburban Heights Medical Center S. C., in Chicago Heights, Illinois—gave remarkably fast, effective, and economical service five times out of five. Waiting times were negligible by comparison with his two experiences with hospital emergency rooms (phlebitis—diagnosed incorrectly as gout—and broken finger). He has since learned a little of how Suburban Heights provides such excellent service. It is a result of policies of quality improvement undertaken initially in the 1970s, long before the acronym "TQM" had been invented. (Since the first draft of this chapter, Roberts's wife, June, has tested Suburban Heights again with a dislocated shoulder. Now it is six out of six for the Robertses.)

Thus, in spite of a generally discouraging level of service quality, we all occasionally encounter examples of high-quality service processes—hospitals, restaurants, hotels, airlines, stores, schools, even government agencies. When we see high quality, it is well worth while to observe carefully and to ask questions to learn how they do it. Ironically, there is something to be learned even from low-quality service processes. Low quality almost always is associated with an insufficient customer orientation, which suggests that other TQM techniques will be ineffective in the absence of a vigorous pursuit of customer satisfaction.

Benchmarking and Exploratory Research

Leading companies have developed sophisticated methodology for benchmarking. However, simple guidelines for getting started on benchmarking, even for novices, can be useful. You must do what should be done in any kind of exploratory research: *You must initially cast a wide net for relevant ideas.* Two initial sources of ideas are knowledgeable people and existing research and background information. Often it is best to start by finding just one knowledgable person who can direct you to both research and background information and, almost always, to other knowledgable people.

You can obtain information from knowledgable people by correspondence, phone calls, or direct meetings. All conversations should be in as much depth as your sources are willing to grant you. You may wish to try to get their permission to tape record the interview, but at the least, you should take detailed notes. Although you would not work from a formal questionnaire, you should have a detailed outline in front of you as you talk. You are likely to find that they are willing to provide information at great length: they're interested in the subject and likely to be flattered by your interest in them. While you are pursuing these conversations, you should also be accumulating background materials, whether suggested by your sources or other research.

You want to make good initial choices about information sources, both organizations and individuals within these organizations. Once you get going, one source leads to another and your sources "snowball." (The term "snowball sampling" has actually been used for this process.) There is no guarantee that you will thereby locate the absolute "best" ideas or practices within your area of interest, but you can hope to assemble a very good collection that will almost surely include better ideas or practices than the ones you started with.

Confidentiality always poses problems, mild or severe, that we cannot treat here. Experience has shown, however, that in the area of TQM, people are willing to share much more information than one would have supposed in advance.

7. INSPECTION AND PERSONAL QUALITY

Because modern TQM stresses prevention of defects rather than weeding them out at final inspection, some people think that all inspections can be eliminated because they are non-value-adding activities. Others believe that inspections are inherently wasteful.

This is not true. Inspections are constraints, but they may be necessary until other constraints have been removed.

One general rule applies to both inspection of the final output of a service or production process and to the results of any intermediate step: Dispense with inspection if and only if you think that the probability of defect is less than a break-even point defined as follows.

> break-even point = unit cost of inspection divided by all costs attributable to a defect, if one occurs

Often this break-even point will be a very small number, such as 0.01, 0.001, or even less, so inspection is indicated. Thus, for example, it is almost always desirable to proofread any document that you write. It would be better if you could prevent all mistakes in the original writing, but for most people the attempt to do this would excessively slow up the process of composition. (In general, when creating something new— say designing prototypes of a new product—excessive concern with error prevention may conflict with the creative process. Error reduction clearly takes first priority only for ongoing activities.)

Again, it is conceivable that removal of some constraint on the writing process, say, somehow learning to proofread as you compose, would make the error rate so low that proofreading could be dispensed with. It is said that Shakespeare never blotted a line of prose; even if true, experience suggests that most of us have not found the secret for rightwriting the first time!

Inspection need not be done by a specialist. You can do it yourself (self-inspection), or your immediate internal customer can do it. From the personal perspective, self-inspection is the rule. You will find that judicious self-inspection can prevent many defects on your personal quality checklist. Just keep in mind the simple formula above for computing the break-even probability of a defect to decide whether a self-inspection is worthwhile.

Finally, inspection can sometimes be automated. Mistake-proofing devices—"poka-yoke"—are procedures that simply make errors impossible, so they can be thought of as 100 percent, completely reliable inspection. (Recall the example of the nozzle for leaded gas not fitting in the gas tank of a car designed to run only on nonleaded gas, and the alarm clock placed across the room to prevent use of the snooze alarm.) In manufacturing, poka-yoke devices are common and cheap. In services, they are harder to come by, but worth seeking.

One simple personal example is to make sure your car keys are in your hand when you push the button to lock your car doors as you get out of your car. Another, mentioned in Chapter 2, is to talk to yourself when you are doing a critical task in order to avoid inattention.

Two Kinds of Waste Removal

1. *Deterministic waste removal:* For example, put the machines closer together to reduce waste of movement or transportation or cut out a totally unnecessary personal activity. Reducing movement or cutting out a totally unnecessary personal activity cannot be harmful.

2. *Expected-value waste removal:* For example, remove an inspection step that is unnecessary if the product is perfect. Cutting out the inspection step may be harmful if too many defects then get through. That is, reducing inspection can cause us to miss a defective unit and to incur costs that would not have been incurred if the inspection had been performed. We thus cut out inspection only if the expected value of inspection is less than its cost.

In particular, we have seen from the above that inspection can be justified by expected-value reasoning under some circumstances—some combination of low cost of inspection, high probability of defect, serious consequences of a defect if one occurs. Inspection is wasteful only if its average cost exceeds the average value of benefits from inspection; in other words, if its expected value is negative.

Of course, if we can drive the probability of a defect to zero, removal of waste is deterministic waste removal—we can't lose. And quality improvements have the general effect of making inspection less valuable.

8. THE CANON FIVE S SYSTEM: HOUSEKEEPING FOR GREATER EFFICIENCY AND REDUCTION OF WASTE

The following description of the Canon Five S system is drawn from the Japanese Management Association's *Canon Production System: Creative Involvement of the Total Workforce* (Productivity Press, 1987). The aim of the system is to reduce waste and to prevent accidents and equipment breakdowns. The Five Ss are initials for Japanese words meaning: proper arrangement, orderliness, cleanliness, cleanup, and discipline. Sometimes "safety" is added. Although the Five S system is designed for implementation by small working groups, it can be adapted to individuals; many Personal Quality Checklists include housekeeping items.

The system is based on the idea that good housekeeping, however some of us may resist it, has economic as well as esthetic value. For example, many people make their beds regularly in the morning even though anything more than a quick straightening out of blankets and sheets is hard to justify on efficiency grounds. By the same token, the extreme cleanliness and orderliness of, say, the Honda plant in Marysville, Ohio, certainly brings intangible benefits.

The system is implemented by a Five S Inspection Sheet, which is much like a Personal Quality Checklist except that it applies to a group and is somewhat longer and more elaborate than most personal checklists.

To illustrate, information on an inspection sheet for a factory is outlined below. There are five general standards. For each general standard, there are five specific standards; as an example, we show one of the specific standards for each of the five general standards.

1. *Proper arrangement* (Sort out unnecessary items)

    ° Have all unnecessary items been removed?

2. *Good order* (A place for everything and everything in its place)

    ° Are work areas uncluttered?

3. *Cleanliness* (Prevent problems by keeping things clean)

  ○ Is clothing neat and clean?

4. *Cleanup* (After-work maintenance and cleanup)

  ○ Are trash cans empty?

5. *Discipline* (Maintaining good habits at Canon)

  ○ Does everyone avoid private conversations during work time?

Canon stresses, "Use your legs and eyes; do regular checks and evaluations." Five S committees, chaired by managers, conduct periodic inspections and look for problem areas.

We believe that good housekeeping for services may be even harder than for manufacturing, but that it would offer comparable benefits. A useful standard for services is the "clean desk rule," which has been included on many Personal Quality Checklists, including that of Sergesketter. However, the standards must be achieved intelligently. If, for example, you achieve your clean desk by sweeping your desk litter into a filing cabinet in the afternoon and bringing it back to your desk the next morning, you are clearly wasting time. *The clean desk should arise as a result of removal of flaws in the underlying work processes.* As we pointed out in Chapter 2, you need to avoid unsystematic and unnecessary paper shuffling. For Roberts the key standard to achieve this was "Putting a small task in a 'hold pile'".

It also works the other way: *The clean desk makes it easier to remove flaws in the underlying work processes.* Thus, by obtaining cleanliness and orderliness on your desk, you reduce wasteful extra movements and searches for misplaced working materials.

The clean desk, important though it is, is still far from the Five S ideal. It does not assure, for example, that there is a place for everything and that everything is in its place. In particular, one's underlying files can be badly disorganized in spite of the clean desk. Only a long-term, systematic reorganization will fix them. (Hint: be *ruthless* in throwing out low-priority materials. Avoid the waste of hanging onto things "just in case.") While the reorganization is going on, you can concentrate on good filing of current materials.

Fortunately, there is a kind of Pareto principle (see the Appendix) that says that one's greatest needs for working materials are concentrated among a relatively few recent items. That principle can help to avert disaster without stopping all current activity in order completely to clean up one's files.

9. PERSONAL QUALITY IN ATHLETICS, FITNESS, AND HEALTH

We begin by citing three simple examples of TQM thinking applied to personal performance in sports, all by Roberts. Each involves simply trying out a new approach ("do" of plan-do-check-act) and seeing if it really works ("check" of PDCA).

EVEN PACING

The first experience came in the early 1940s, before Roberts knew anything about TQM (the term "TQM" dates back only to the 1980s). In middle-distance running races in high school and college, he learned from painful experience that a fast start always led to an agonizing slowing down for the balance of a race. However, the coaching wisdom of the time always called for starting very fast and hoping that eventually one could learn to maintain the pace all the way. (A more refined version was that one should go out fast, slow down in the middle of the race, and then sprint at the end.)

Eventually, a distaste for suffering led Roberts to experiment with a more reasonable starting pace. In his next cross-country race, a three-mile run, he was dead last at the end of the first quarter mile in a time of 75 seconds; the leaders ran it in about 60 seconds. (Had they been able to maintain that pace, they would have run the first of the three miles in 4:00 minutes, which then would have been a world's record for the *one*-mile run.) For the rest of the race, he passed runners steadily and ended up in the middle of the pack, not because he speeded up but because the others slowed down. Subsequently, his performance relative to other runners was much improved.

In recent decades, even pacing has become the generally accepted practice. Most world distance records are nearly evenly paced.

Decades afterwards, as an age-group runner, Roberts was able to validate the youthful experiment. In marathons, he discovered that an even *slightly* too-fast pace (as little as 5–10 seconds per mile) for the first 20 miles was punished by agony and drastic slowing in the final 10 kilometers. The overall marathon time suffered. In his best marathons, he ran at an even pace all the way and actually was only pleasantly tired in the final 10 kilometers, when he was able to pass hundreds of runners who had run the first 20 miles too fast.

DRINKING AND RUNNING

During age-group running in the early 1980s, Roberts noticed a severe degradation of running times, even when, as recommended, he drank substantial amounts of fluid at aid stations during races in hot weather. He noticed also that drinking during the race resulted in feelings of mild nausea and sluggishness. He reasoned that the real imperative was to keep the body temperature low, and that there was a better way to do it: supersaturate with large intakes of fluid and soak running clothes just before the start, then douse oneself thoroughly with water at every aid station and at every other opportunity as well. (It is useful, but not essential, to avoid soaking one's socks and shoes.)

Hence, contrary to all advice, he decided to try to avoid drinking any fluid during hot weather races, even in marathons. Admittedly he launched this experiment with trepidation, and started with shorter races. If he were wrong, the consequences could be much more serious than a slow running time. However, he knew that there is plenty of early warning of heat exhaustion: one stops sweating.

Races from 10K to marathons confirmed not only that he had no problem with heat exhaustion, but that his hot-weather running times were now consistently much closer to the times made at the same distances in cool weather.

LONG TRAINING RUNS

Finally, Roberts discovered that it is unnecessary to do long training runs before marathons. During the five months before his best marathon, in 1982, he simply trained six miles a day, seven days a week (except for races), at a pace that was brisk for a person of his age, slightly under seven minutes per mile. He ran steadily at a 7:05 pace through that marathon.

TQM for Improving Technique

The quickest opportunities for TQM in improving athletic performance come in matters of technique. To improve technique, you have to have ideas about alternatives to current techniques. In personal projects in

Roberts's classes, students have often come up with these ideas when recording and analyzing the results of regular practice. Popular subjects have been free-throw and three-point shooting in basketball, tennis service, place kicking, archery, target shooting, skeet shooting, swimming, cycling, and golf.

In most of these studies, the students' performance has been in a state of statistical control during the base period, and statistical control at a higher level has been achieved by alteration of technique. The example of putting improvement in Section 1 is one illustration. Another illustration was free-throw shooting. The student went from being in control at a success rate of 75 percent to being in control at a success rate of 82 percent, mainly by shifting the aim point and changing the arch.

Sometimes it may be possible to do genuine experiments on technique. That is, the sequence of the techniques being considered can be mixed up, instead of just making a single transition from one to the other, as was done in the examples of putting and free throws. A freestyle swimmer, for example, might experiment with two degrees of body roll, normal and exaggerated. In a given workout, each successive lap could be timed. In each pair of successive laps, one would be with normal body roll and the other with exaggerated roll. The toss of a coin could determine which was tried first in each pair of laps. The mean of the differences in times—exaggerated roll versus normal—for each pair of laps is an estimate of the merit of the exaggerated roll relative to the normal. A positive mean difference favors the exaggerated roll, a negative mean difference favors the standard roll. A simple statistical test helps to decide whether the difference is significant.

TQM for Training Methods and Diet

In sports generally and endurance sports in particular, there is great interest in the possibility of improving performance through better training methods and better diet. Unfortunately, the effects of either of these approaches are likely to be felt only after substantial periods of time, that is, the effects are lagged. By contrast, a technique change, once perfected, registers its full effect each time it is applied.

Thus, in learning about the effects of training methods and diet, we have to try out major changes for substantial periods in time, on the order of weeks or months rather than days. There have been many interesting examples in distance running. Arthur Lydiard, a New Zealand runner and coach of Peter Snell and other leading runners, was one of the early pioneers in trying out, both for himself and his runners, training mileage much in excess of what was thought necessary before 1950. His basic training schedule was the same for all runners from the 800 meters to the marathon. While the details differed from month to month, it entailed running roughly 100 miles a week, in contrast to typical training regimens of 10 to 15 miles a week in the 1930s. Much of the improvement of running times since 1950 can be attributed to these training volumes. Runners from Lydiard's area of New Zealand won several Olympic medals in the 1950s and 1960s.

Lydiard reasoned that if 100 miles per week were good, 200 miles a week would be better, so he tried it out himself for several weeks. It became obvious that 200 miles a week was worse—he was just generally exhausted and performance deteriorated—so Lydiard abandoned experimentation along these lines. Many runners have since tried to force training mileage upwards and have run into similar problems, including serious stress injuries.

TQM for Prevention and Treatment of Injuries

Stress injuries (gradual onset) are a very serious hazard in running and in many other athletic activities, such as gymnastics. Traumatic injuries (sudden onset) are correspondingly important in football and basketball. Proper management of injuries is essential.

The old paradigm for dealing with stress injuries was simple: "You got it running. Run it out! Run through the pain!" This paradigm is now generally discredited. What has happened is that a variety of people with interests in sports medicine have combined their own experiences and, consciously or not, used the simple problem-solving tools of TQM to lead to very useful insights. Essentially it is the Japanese "Five Whys," continually probing back in the chain of causation to get at root causes. Cause-and-effect diagrams may be helpful also.

Everything is connected: what appears to be a knee problem may arise from overpronating feet and may be corrected by shoe inserts or "orthotics." Pronation is the sideways rolling over of the foot when it strikes. This rolling over imparts a twist to the knee joint. If the pronation is excessive, cumulative damage to the knee joint, "chondromalacia," can occur.

One good example is that of a runner who, before the era of common use of orthotics, suffered intermittent pain in one knee. He noticed that the pain occurred when running on one side of the road but not the other. It occurred to him that the slant of the road could be simulated by a shoe insert. He devised such an insert and the problem went away.

Many runners have found that cross-training provides an invaluable aid to rehabilitation of running injuries. Very few running injuries, for example, prevent walking, biking, or swimming. Even though some specific running fitness is lost temporarily, these substitute activities maintain general aerobic and muscular fitness and the healing of the injury is speeded.

Improvement of Fitness and Health

A closely related topic is that of fitness and health. Many of Roberts's students have followed systematic programs to improve fitness or strength and have benefited from the use of statistical methods to monitor progress. Essentially, as in TQM, they define and map an improvement process and record key inputs and process measurements in time ordered sequence. The run chart is the primary tool. A substantial degree of success is virtually guaranteed, and the data reinforce and guide the whole experience.

One surprise is how much fitness can be achieved with limited inputs over short periods of time. In most instances improvement is still occurring at the end of an 11-week course: the students have not reached the flattening-out stage when the only problem is to hold the gains via control charting.

Some have included health standards on their checklists—for example, avoidance of certain foods or of smoking. Individuals can also use other quality techniques to maintain health. For example, hypertensive individuals can monitor their own blood pressures and diabetics can monitor their blood sugar levels; we have had students who have done this and we present an example in the Appendix. Again, the run chart is the primary tool, but with additional training, students can make good use of control charts. For diabetics, in particular, the control charts can provide early warning of health disturbances.

10. PROCESS MAPPING

One of the best ways to understand a process is to "map" it. This will show the steps that are necessary to do the work, the order in which the steps are completed, and who does each step. In most instances, just mapping the process will provide insights into how to improve the process. However, there is still more to be gained from mapping, because the map provides a template for determining where standards should be set regarding accuracy and cycle time. Once standards are in place, defects can be counted and cycle time can be measured. With the data from these measurements, quality improvement techniques can be effectively used to insure continuous improvement.

In the review of process maps, one area of great opportunity for improvement lies in reducing those instances where there are handoffs between individuals or organizations. As a general rule, these are where most defects and delays occur. To learn how to work with process maps, identify a key process that you use *personally* and map it. The following example illustrates how to map the process of responding to a request for information in writing.

Start the mapping process by identifying the purpose. In this instance, the purpose is to "respond to a request for information with a one- to two-page memorandum." Write the purpose and draw a box below it with a column for each individual or organization involved in the process you wish to improve (see Figure 3). At the top of each column, name the individual or organization who performs work during the process.

To the left of the box identify the input (request for information) and below the input list the suppliers of that input (customers and associates). Then describe each step in the process in the column where the work is completed. Draw a box around each of these steps and use arrows to designate the work flows. Identify the output (response to request) next to the lower right portion of the chart along with the "customers" of the process (customers and associates). In this illustration the suppliers and the customers are the same people, but this is not usually the case.

At this point you will want to identify your customers' expectations in terms of accuracy and cycle time. It is reasonable to assume that zero errors is the standard for accuracy. Standards for cycle time can be established by asking each requester how soon a response is expected. Your goal is then to exceed expectations so that you may "delight the customer."

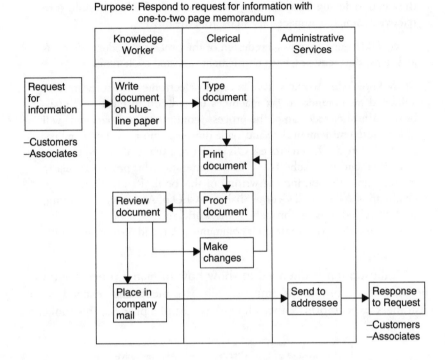

Figure 3 Process A

A good place to count defects regarding accuracy is the "review document" step. If a number of defects occur here, they should be categorized to determine what is causing the largest number, then the second largest, third largest, and so on. This is the basic idea of Pareto analysis. Quality improvement analysis and tools can then be used to seek out and remove root causes, starting with the most frequent category of defect and working down. Thus you will be working on the most important problems in the proper sequence.

Cycle time is measured from the time the request is made until the requester has the response, including time in transit. A component of cycle time is *entitlement time,* the actual time it takes to perform the work step. For example, the entitlement time to print a two-page document might be one minute. In Process A (Figure 3), measurement of cycle time will usually show a wide distribution ranging from four hours for a "rush" document to two weeks or even more. You will probably find that your process needs improvement in order to meet the expectations of the requester in most instances. One way to improve is to measure the cycle time versus entitlement time between different steps in the process, with the aim of reducing wasteful steps. A better approach when feasible, is to remove completely unnecessary steps from the process.

Process B (Figure 4) shows a redesign of the process to reduce handoffs and steps, thus reducing both entitlement time and cycle time.

Many knowledge workers have access to electronic mail software that will send memoranda to fax machines in addition to electronic mailboxes. A further redesign of the process (continuous improvement) will reduce both entitlement time and cycle time even more, as shown in Process C (Figure 5). When Process C is used, cycle time is driven very close to entitlement time. Roberts and Sergesketter used this process regularly in communicating during the writing of this book. Randy Tobias, vice chairman of AT&T, and George Shaheen, CEO of Andersen Consulting, both travel extensively throughout the world and use a variation of this process in order to facilitate their communications and be more effective.

This illustration is intended to show how to map a process and use the map for continuous improvement to meet and exceed your customers' expectations. Since all work is part of a process, this tool can

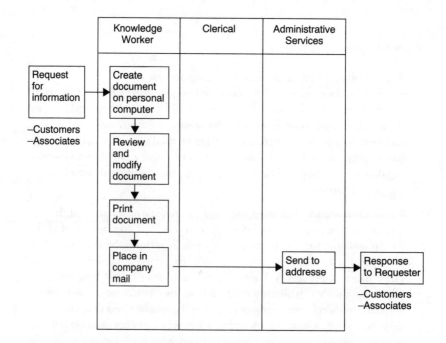

Figure 4 Process B

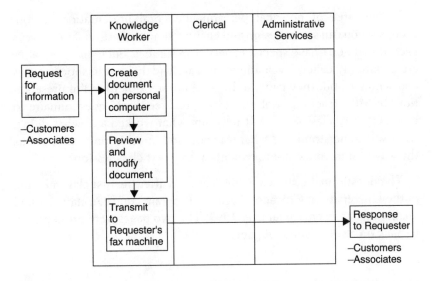

Figure 5 Process C

be applied to all the work that you do and thus aid you in your efforts to improve quality.

Various graphical devices can be used to map processes from different perspectives. A common term for these mapping devices is "flowchart." Flowcharts can often bring rapid improvement by making obvious what steps can be eliminated altogether, as in Processes B and C of our example. Measurement of cycle times for certain components of an overall process can show where the greatest delays are occurring.

11. SIMPLE QUESTIONNAIRES

Exceeding customer expectations and evaluation of customer satisfaction are central to TQM. In many instances, simple questions posed in conversation will quickly establish a customer's expectations and how well they are being satisfied. But when there are many customers, possibly dispersed over a wide geographic area, more formal means of questioning are needed. These are often called surveys. Questionnaires of various types come into play, and, usually, sampling is needed. Conducting a survey of substantial scope requires technical knowledge about questionnaire design, sampling, processing of completed forms, and statistical summarization and analysis.

In one area of personal performance—oral presentations before groups—you can safely design and analyze simple questionnaire surveys even if you don't have special expertise in surveys. Such questionnaires are commonly called "evaluations" and are widely used in short courses and seminars, but they can also be used for any other kind of presentation. In MBA teaching, Roberts uses a "fast-feedback" questionnaire to evaluate every class session. It tells him what worked and what didn't, what was understood and what was not, and, most importantly, points the way to immediate improvements at the next class session.

The questionnaire shown below was used after the first class meeting of the University of Chicago Executive Program course in statistics and quality management, in January 1992. The two pages were printed back to back on a single sheet of paper.

FAST-FEEDBACK QUESTIONNAIRE FOR BUS. 520-88, CLASS OF WEEK ONE, WINTER, 1992

TODAY'S CLASS:

	Little or Nothing		A Fair Amount		A Great Deal
Overall, how much did you get out of today's class?	1	2	3	4	5

What was the most important thing you learned?

What was the muddiest point?

What single change by the instructor would have most improved this class?

Please comment briefly on the helpfulness of the advance reading assignments for today's class.

YOUR PREPARATION FOR TODAY'S CLASS:

	Little or Nothing		A Fair Amount		A Great Deal
Overall, how much did you get out of your preparation for today's class?	1	2	3	4	5

What one thing can *the instructor do* to help you to improve your future class preparations?

What one thing can *you do* to help improve your future class preparations?

YOUR PROGRESS ON QUALITY IMPROVEMENT PROJECTS:

	Behind Schedule		On Schedule		Ahead of Schedule
On balance, how are you doing on your quality improvement projects?*					
Project 1	1	2	3	4	5
Project 2	1	2	3	4	5

What one thing can *the instructor do* to help you to make better progress on the projects?

What one thing can *you do* to help you to make better progress on the projects?

*Note: Students had received an advance assignment to get started on these projects.

GENERAL

Any other feedback about any aspect of the course, including use of computing or topics that you would like to hear more about?

Are you having problems unrelated to this course that the instructor should be aware of?

Notice that there are two types of questions. First is the simple scaled response such as:

	Little or Nothing		A Fair Amount		A Great Deal
Overall, how much did you get out of today's class?	1	2	3	4	5

Second is the simple free-response question such as: "What was the most important thing you learned?"

No computer is needed to make the analysis. The scaled responses can be quickly sorted into piles, and the frequencies for each of the five categories can then be counted. The answers to the free-response questions can simply be read; if more formal analysis is desired, you can group them into similar response categories and count the number in each (Pareto analysis again, see the Appendix) to determine which categories are most common and thus have highest claim on corrective action.

For the class of 80 students, it took Roberts a little over an hour to determine the weaknesses and strengths of his presentation. Among other things, he learned:

- At times he did not speak loudly enough to be easily heard in the large classroom. Subsequently, he wore a portable microphone.
- Most of the students had done and liked the advance reading on quality management, but they felt that Roberts spent too much

time in class reviewing material in the reading. He concluded that he could reduce actual class time on topics in quality management, thus leaving more time for topics in statistics, for which the students felt that they needed more help in class.

Questions on the feedback questionnaire were varied from class meeting to class meeting, depending on the topics to be covered. Quickly the questionnaire was reduced to a single side of one sheet of paper. Here is an example.

FAST-FEEDBACK QUESTIONNAIRE FOR BUS. 520-88, CLASS OF WEEK NINE, WINTER, 1992

	Little or Nothing		A Fair Amount		A Great Deal
Overall, how much did you get out of today's class?	1	2	3	4	5

What was the muddiest point?

	Very Insecure		Moderately Secure		Very Secure
Overall, how secure are you in your understanding of statistics?	1	2	3	4	5

Comments?

	Very Insecure		Moderately Secure		Very Secure
Overall, how secure are you in your understanding of TQM?	1	2	3	4	5

Comments?

	Little or No Help		Fairly Helpful		Very Helpful
How do you evaluate the instructor's response to your feedback forms?	1	2	3	4	5

Any other feedback about *any* aspect of the course?

Feedback questionnaires like these are easy to construct; you don't have to be a survey expert to do them. Here are some guidelines:

- Prepare a formal questionnaire. This is much better than asking the audience to scribble suggestions on a sheet of scratch paper.
- Keep the questionnaire simple and short. It should take no more than five minutes to fill it out.
- Aim at 100 percent response. The five-minute time for filling out the questionnaire should come out of the actual presentation time; it should not be a task to be accomplished as the audience is leaving the meeting.
- Read the questionnaires immediately and do any simple tabulations that are needed.
- If feasible, give the audience quick feedback on your analysis of their responses. In the context of a course, this reverse feedback can be extremely valuable. For example, "muddy points" can be cleared up quickly and effectively. We find that when we give full written feedback, most students will read and appreciate it; a second channel of communication, outside of formal class sessions, is thereby opened up.

Questionnaire surveys are useful for measuring customer satisfaction in many service areas. As the scope of desired information gets broader, the very simple type of questionnaire shown here may suffice up to a point, but it is often desirable to get expert assistance on the design of the questionnaire. Also, when sampling is indicated, it is well to get help on the design of the sample.

Warning: Beware of haphazard customer sampling and low response rates. The information thus obtained may be very misleading; for example, it may give undue emphasis to customers at the extremes of satisfaction, those most pleased and those most disgruntled. A disgruntled customer provides useful information, but it is not helpful to have a distorted impression of how many disgruntled customers there are.

12. PERSONAL VISION, MISSION, AND VALUES

Many organizations engaged in the pursuit of TQM find it useful to set down their fundamental goals and objectives. What at first sounds like an exercise in reaffirmation of motherhood and apple pie turns out to be genuinely helpful as a guide for the never-ending TQM journey.

We show examples by Motorola and the Central Region of AT&T. Both are printed on the two sides of a small plastic card that can be easily carried by all employees (on p. 102 the other sides are shown).

OUR FUNDAMENTAL OBJECTIVE
(Everyone's Overriding Responsibility)

Total Customer Satisfaction

 *MOTOROLA*

OUR VISION
To be recognized by our customers and our employees as the global leader in information technology.

EVERY EMPLOYEE'S
OVERRIDING RESPONSIBILITY

- Delight the Customer
- Devotion to Quality

Central Region

KEY BELIEFS—*how we will always act*

- Constant Respect for People
- Uncompromising Integrity

KEY GOALS—*what we must accomplish*

- Best in Class
  - —*People*
  - —*Marketing*
  - —*Technology*
  - —*Product: Software, Hardware and Systems*
  - —*Manufacturing*
  - —*Service*
- Increased Global Market Share
- Superior Financial Results

KEY INITIATIVES—*how we will do it*

- Six Sigma Quality
- Total Cycle Time Reduction
- Product, Manufacturing and Environmental Leadership
- Profit Improvement
- Empowerment for all, in a Participative, Cooperative and Creative Workplace

Rev. 8-92

OUR VALUES

- **Respect for individuals**
- **Dedication to helping customers**
- **Highest standards of integrity**
- **Innovation**
- **Teamwork**

WE WILL ALWAYS:

- **Act in accordance with our values**
- **Be responsive to customers & employees**
- **Learn more about our business**
- **Act Professionally**
- **Be Honest**
- **Meet and follow up on our commitments**
- **Coach, support, empower and involve each other**
- **Thank our customers for their business**

AT&T QUALITY PRINCIPLES

- **The customer comes first**
- **Quality happens through people**
- **All work is part of a process**
- **Suppliers are an integral part of our business**
- **Prevention is achieved through planning**
- **Quality improvement never ends**

Sergesketter's Personal Vision, Mission, and Values

It occurred to us that the same careful reflection that can lead to organizational statements like those by Motorola and AT&T can well be applied at the personal level. As you think about preparing your Personal Quality Checklist, it can help to set down your personal *vision*, your personal *mission statement*, and your personal *values*. When Sergesketter was a lad of ten, his family physician outlined a vision for him which he adopted. His *vision statement* is:

I will endeavor to lead a balanced life, spending my time and attention in the areas of the four points of the cross below.

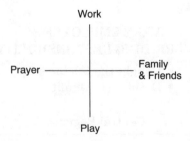

His *mission statement* is:

> To lead a rich spiritual life and to conduct myself in a highly ethical manner in all matters; to love and care for the members of my family to the best of my abilities; to perform my work with the highest quality and to treat my associates with respect; to maintain friendships that bring about joy and happiness; to maintain my health through proper diet and exercise; to play and to have fun on a regular basis; and to not take myself too seriously.

Sergesketter's *value statement* is:

> I commit to these values to guide my decisions and behavior.
> *Respect for others:* Treat all other people with respect and dignity at all times.
> *Integrity:* Honesty in all of my dealings with others and with myself.
> *Commitment:* Application of my energies and capabilities to the people and organizations to whom I have an obligation.
> *Excellence:* Always endeavor to be the best I can be.

Writing down your own personal statements will help you to create your initial Personal Quality Checklist, serve as a guide as you modify your list down the road, and provide an excellent opportunity to reflect on the things that are most important in your life.

13. PERSONAL PROCESS MANAGEMENT

After a year of experience with the Personal Quality Checklist, Roberts—like Sergesketter—was getting very few defects. Lateness for meetings was his most intractable standard because it is only partly controllable at the personal level. The main task now was to hold the gains. The checklist does that without much burden: if there are few defects, it's easy to record them!

As a result of using the checklist, Roberts became increasingly aware of opportunities for further improvement. He found himself looking over his own shoulder as he worked, combining actual work with simultaneous observation of it. As a result, he began to view what he was doing as it would be seen by an outside observer. Can this idea be exploited for further improvement? Can you manage your own work processes?

Some work activity is uncontrollable in any substantial way by the individual: a phone call must be answered, a meeting must be attended, an airplane must be caught. But a great deal of activity is at least partly controllable. Thus, while observing his own work, Roberts began to analyze his controllable activities in the light of total quality principles, especially principles for the reduction of waste. As a result, he found himself modifying his work behavior while working. Here are some evolving guidelines for doing this:

° Keep scheduling your work, and revising the schedule if necessary, for the next few minutes, hours, or days: when there's a choice of tasks to be tackled, think consciously of the sequence in which they will be approached.

° Keep thinking of ways to do repeated tasks more efficiently. For example, Roberts observed that keeping track of essential materials for current projects—for example, teaching materials, handouts, and student papers for a current class—had become increasingly difficult as the number of projects had recently expanded. Consequently, while actually working, he has been developing a better *current filing system*.

° His previous filing system was to accumulate materials for small projects unsystematically in file folders; for big projects, in piles. This means that nothing relevant to the current project is lost, but it can be slow to retrieve. He came to realize that maintaining a strict chronological sequence of the materials within each folder or pile makes quick retrieval easier.

° This is not a new idea, of course; many years ago, one of Roberts's first bosses, Neal Gilliatt, applied it. But the current application is new to Roberts. If he had benchmarked on Neal Gilliatt, he would have saved an enormous amount of time over the intervening years.

° With each new job input—e.g., letter, phone call, reading material—consider *consciously* what your appropriate response should be. Should reading material, for example, be skimmed now or immediately discarded. If skimmed, should it be read carefully at a later time? If read carefully, should it be kept? If kept, what is the best way to file it so that it can be found when needed in the future?

° Look for small rearrangements of your own working area, efficient planning of small errands and chores, or opportunistic fitting-in of background tasks, like picking up your mail.

° On all manual tasks, watch yourself to see opportunities for improvement. For example, watch how you manipulate floppy disks on your PC.

° Consciously work at making quick responses to unexpected demands on your time. This relates to the general TQM principle that, since consumer demands are often very hard to forecast, it may be more useful to work on quick response than to try to develop better forecasts.

° *In doing all this, you should be simultaneously talking to yourself, usually silently.*

Thus, in addition to thinking about *what* you are doing, you must simultaneously think about *how* you are doing it and *how* you could do it better, either right now or the next time you face the same task. That is, you must think about your *job methodology* as well as your *job tasks.*

Sergesketter terms this approach *personal process management.* He has applied the idea for several years to his tennis game. He learned from Tim Gallwey's book (W. Timothy Gallwey, *The Inner Game of Tennis* [New York: Random House, 1974]) that saying "bounce" when the ball bounces and "hit" when the racket hits the ball enhances his concentration on the game. Consequently, his strokes are much smoother and he keeps the ball in play longer, which statistically is an advantage because it gives the other player more opportunities to make an error and lose the point.

The "calming effect" of personal process management is comparable to that noted in Chapter 2 for the Personal Quality Checklist itself. When you are concentrating on how to improve your work methodology, you are less likely to get flustered because you are anxious about the outcome of what you are doing. You concentrate on playing the game rather than watching the scoreboard. You can hope for rapid initial improvement.

Personal process management has another potential contribution: it can make dull tasks interesting.

It would be possible to make personal process management into a standard on your checklist, but we recommend keeping it separate from the checklist itself. See the discussion on "Loss of Concentration" near the end of Section 4 of Chapter 2, where we suggest a numerical scaling of the success of each day's efforts.

Another approach, suggested by Professor Selwyn Becker of the University of Chicago, is to keep a log in which you can note observations about your personal work processes, as well as concentration lapses and what led to them. Reflection on your log may lead to useful changes.

Retrospective Personal Process Management

Francis Fullam of the University of Chicago Medical Center has recently had the experience of working with an administrator who was so overloaded that she didn't see how she could find time for TQM activities. Fullam sat down with her to go over her calendar for the previous week and her recollection of activities not recorded on the calendar. They classified all indentifiable activities, such as meetings and report writing, into one of the following categories:

1. Totally unnecessary activity: no one would ever notice if it were discontinued, no rationale for hidden benefits that might not be noticed.
2. Activity that can be done in less time: for example, one routine meeting was allocated one hour per week, regardless of the agenda. It was found that 30 minutes was adequate.
3. Activity that can be delegated: someone else could do it equally well with a little practice and would benefit from the added challenge.
4. All other.

The result was about eleven hours per week were immediately freed up. Still more time could of course be freed up using other personal quality tools described in this book.

---

14. STATISTICAL WORK SAMPLING

For decades, industrial engineers have used work sampling as one route to the understanding and improvement of work processes. The time-study expert with stopwatch and clipboard who times each step of a machining operation is a familiar stereotype.

Statistical work sampling is a variant of this general idea in which unobtrusive "snap" readings are taken at randomly chosen moments in order to see what activity is being carried out. By averaging many snap readings, one can get a good statistical picture of work activity. For example, it might turn out that factory workers were spending 15 percent of their time waiting for work to come to them.

The idea of statistical work sampling has been applied to TQM by Tim Fuller (mentioned above in Section 4) in a classic article, "Eliminating Complexity from Work: Improving Productivity by Enhancing Quality," *National Productivity Review* (Autumn 1985, 327–344). In Fuller's approach, individuals apply statistical work sampling to themselves and the results are pooled in order to get a picture of aggregate organizational activity.

Fuller focuses on determining how much time is spent on activities that can be classified as "complexity," by which he means steps that would not be necessary if an ideal flowchart for the process were in effect. The *actual* flowchart includes these additional steps that give it a "complex" appearance. Thus, complexity really means any task that is necessary only because of previous flaws in the implementation of the process. The most common example of complexity is rework because of poor quality, but it could include dealing with customer complaints, processing returned goods, or recalling a product to correct a problem.

FULLER'S APPROACH TO STATISTICAL WORK SAMPLING

The advent of cheap, multifunction electronic watches has made work sampling simple and easy for almost anyone to do. The basic idea is to look periodically at what a person is doing so that a list of activities can be developed and the relative frequency of each measured. If we ignore non-work-related activities, the list can be sorted into two categories of real work and complexity due to *external* problems.

Then subactivities can be similarly grouped into real work and complexity related to *internal* process errors. When these data have been prepared, management can pull together interdepartmental task groups to eliminate the external errors. Work group improvement teams led by a supervisor can address the internal problems by solving the ones over which they have control and collecting data on the others so that management can take the appropriate action.

Fuller's approach can be readily adapted by individuals to personal quality improvement. Here's how it would be done:

Procure a watch that has a "repeating countdown" function. This function allows setting a countdown timer to a particular number of minutes and seconds. When the countdown feature is turned on, the watch counts down to zero, beeps one or more times, resets itself automatically, and begins the countdown again. [With some watches, after resetting, you must press a button to start another countdown.]

. . . Each time the employee hears the beep, he or she is to immediately stop working and make several entries in his or her log or check sheet. The employee should record the time, place, activity, and subactivity.

This procedure will be most successful if a list of the major activities is determined in advance so that sorting will be easy. . . . In general, the more activities that a person might be doing, the more observations are required to obtain a true picture of what the person is working on. In most cases 100 should be enough for one person. . . .

It is important that the beep of the watch be a surprise. . . . If the employee anticipates the beep, he or she is likely to modify his or her behavior in some way that will distort the data. Ideally, the turning on and turning off times of the watch should be random. But since few watches have the capability to generate random beeps, the countdown timer should be set at an interval long enough so the individual will be surprised when it beeps. Good results have been obtained with settings of twenty-three, forty-one, and forty-seven minutes but not with sixty minutes.

No matter what the setting, subjects are bound to change their behavior to some degree because of the study. However, this is potentially beneficial if the person is permanently imbued with an interest in studying the activities being performed.

Fuller's studies often show that a very small fraction of work time is taken up by "real work"; a fraction as low as 15 percent or even 5 percent is common. This is the penalty exacted by internal and external complexity. When the goal is personal quality improvement, the complexity coming from the rest of the organization is not controllable by the individual. An additional category would be needed for complexity caused by the individual's own past activities. Work sampling can thus direct the individual's attention to personal work flaws that lead to complexity.

Fuller's approach is a simple way, requiring no new accounting methodology, to get an idea of the potential improvement in an organization from a TQM effort.

Statistical work sampling can be directed to other classifications of activities than complexity. You might, for example, want to get some idea of how much of your time is spent in various activities, such as correspondence, meetings, filling out government forms, presentations, errands, meeting customers, or talking with direct reports.

5

BEYOND PERSONAL QUALITY

1. MORE ON TOTAL QUALITY MANAGEMENT

In Chapter 1 we introduced many salient ideas of Total Quality Management (TQM). In this chapter we expand these ideas and then show the connection between the foundation of personal quality given in this book and the issues and problems arising when an organization tries to embrace the principles of TQM. In doing so, we hope to accomplish two objectives:

1. Build on personal quality to provide a fuller glimpse of organizational quality. TQM.
2. Set forth ideas of organizational quality that may be helpful in improving personal quality.

We do not aim to provide a full introduction to TQM, but we want to provide some background for readers who have not previously encountered it. Readers who are familiar with TQM or who are interested mainly in personal quality can skip the first four sections.

TQM as a Union of Diverse Constituents

TQM embraces several broad constituents that can and should be mutually reinforcing. The following list is incomplete, but suggestive of the range of activities and ideas that go into TQM.

1. *Quality control*, applied throughout the organization, both for production and service activities; for example:

- Inspection
- Statistical Process Control
- Elementary management tools: e.g., flowcharts, cause-and-effect analysis, check sheets, questionnaires, Pareto analysis, time series plots, scatter plots, histograms, stratification.

- ° Sophisticated statistical tools such as design of experiments and intervention analysis.
- ° Systematic approaches to quality improvement, such as Plan-Do-Check-Act (PDCA) or Plan-Do-Study-Act; the Diagnostic Journey and Remedial Journey; Kume's Q Story; and Focus-PDCA.
- ° "Zero defects" or "Zero variation": focusing attention on better ways to conform to quality specifications, in part by motivation not to produce defects.
- ° Robust design of processes and products.
- ° Reliability

2. *Just-In-Time (JIT) and related ideas:* for simplification, elimination of waste or removal of constraints, and building flexibility and fast response into all processes and into the design of new products and processes. JIT is applicable to service processes as well as manufacturing processes. The world is now moving beyond JIT to a broader concept sometimes called "time-based management," with emphasis on elimination of waste time—largely queue and rework time. Basic concurrent engineering (see point 8, below) can be thought of as the application of the same principles to product development.

3. *Employee involvement:* harnessing the knowledge and creative powers of all employees, individually and in small teams; usually aims at a complete transformation of organizational culture and has major implications for organizational structure. Training and education are essential. It is important to drive out fear of making suggestions for change, trying out new methods, being blamed for problems that are inherent in the system, or losing one's job because of quality improvements. Some typical elements:

- ° Empowerment, the authority to plan and do the work you are capable of doing
- ° Self-managed work teams, an example of empowerment
- ° "Market in" or "market pull" orientation
- ° Learning organization
- ° Customer-managed organization
- ° Personal quality improvement

4. *Total customer satisfaction:* searching out better ways to serve all customers, internal as well as external, even going beyond "satisfaction"

to "delight." Emphasizes customer-driven measurements, as defined by customers' wants and needs. Of all the TQM constituents, this has a unique claim: If one started from focus on customer satisfaction, one would be led to the rest of TQM.

5. *Benchmarking:* "steal and improve on any good idea that isn't proprietary, *whatever the source of the idea."* Get rid of the "not-invented-here" syndrome. Potential problem: customer wants may not be fully met by anyone in the market.

6. *Stretch objectives:* rapid deployment *throughout an organization* of efforts to lower error rates, cycle times, and costs for key processes by establishing core competencies and removing constraints on improvement. Requires identification of customer/supplier relations, internal and external, and process mapping. Stresses rates of improvement rather than absolute attainment, thus making possible valid comparisons of progress between different subunits of an organization. Underlying this approach is the basic idea that continuous improvement can embrace large improvements as well as small ones: illustrations are Schaffer's "Breakthrough Strategy" (see Section 6, below), Hammer's "Reengineering," and General Electric's "Workout."

7. *Hoshin Planning:* systematic procedures for achieving the aims of traditional Management by Objectives (MBO), but relating objectives to what can realistically be achieved and inviting participation of all levels of the organization in setting objectives. Relies heavily on data on customer needs, competitors' capabilities, and internal process capabilities. Often uses the "Seven Management Tools"—such as affinity diagrams—in helping groups to reach creative consensus.

8. *Simultaneous engineering, concurrent engineering:* cooperation for development of new products, with emphasis on fast and frequent prototyping and other ideas for reducing the cycle time of new product development. Translation of customers needs into new products and processes is aided by Quality Function Deployment (QFD) and Taguchi engineering ideas about robust design. All involved in the development are empowered to come in the process early, start anticipating and planning their roles, and making suggestions that may help other departments.

9. *The new management:* replacement of top-down control through accounting numbers by leadership of senior management for improvement of processes with the ultimate aim of better bottom-line results.

Harmonizes with such elements as Hoshin Planning and Quality Function Deployment, but can arise independently. Leads to major changes in organizational structure, flattened organization charts, and reduced emphasis on types of control such as remote top-down control using accounting numbers that encourage tampering with processes and manipulation of appearances rather than improvement of processes.

10. *Operational standards for organizational excellence,* as illustrated, for example, by the criteria of the Malcolm Baldrige National Quality Award.

11. *Process management and improvement:* A process is a series of activities by which inputs are converted to outputs. The activities are definable, repeatable, measurable, and predictable. Process management is a methodology that attempts continually to increase effectiveness and efficiency of processes. This requires detailed analysis of the processes to reduce cycle times and defects and to improve customer satisfaction. By defining and documenting processes we can better understand:

- ° What we do
- ° How we link together
- ° What our dependencies are
- ° Which activities are redundant and therefore unnecessary
- ° How we can simplify what we do
- ° How to continuously improve

The keys to the success of process management are: management commitment and involvement, identification of critical success factors, and a cross-functional focus.

2. IDEAS OF TOTAL QUALITY MANAGEMENT

To flesh out the outlines just given, we now spell out ideas that are widely accepted by advocates of Total Quality Management.

FUNDAMENTALS

- ° Consistent orientation toward pleasing customers, internal or external. Quality is thus customer defined.
- ° Visualization of an organization as a system of interdependent pro-

cesses, each with suppliers and customers, that can be mapped by
flowcharts and process maps.
° Goals for all processes, manufacturing or service: high quality and
  productivity, in a state of statistical control (predictable in terms of
  probability), short cycle time, small lot sizes, low inventories, fast
  changeovers, just-in-time processing, total preventive maintenance
  (TPM), low costs, and elimination of mistakes and waste.
° Measurement and scientific method, including statistics, applied
  for improvement of processes through the organization. ("In God
  we trust; all others must bring data.")
° Aggressive but realistic improvement targets for all products, processes, and services. Improvement can be continuous (many small
  changes) *and* discontinuous (occasional major breakthroughs), and
  it should be never ending: it's always possible to do better.
° "Robust new product design": a major objective is to create products that will still perform well when used under unfavorable condi-
  tions.
° Retain the gains from past improvements. (This is the traditional
  American "quality control" or "quality assurance," which is only one
  component of TQM.)

HUMAN RESOURCES AND ORGANIZATION

° Continuing education and training; expansion of job scope and en-
  richment of careers.
° Teamwork: work teams (or QC circles) within departments and
  special improvement teams from different departments and organizational levels, for improving cross-functional cooperation and
  solving interdepartmental problems. Teams can often accomplish
  more than their individual members can do on their own.
° Opportunities and incentives for all employees to buy into organizational goals: employee involvement.
° Employment stability.
° Flat organization charts; simple, structured, documented designs
  for all products and processes.
° Alignment of quality objectives of each subunit of a larger organization.
° Automation only when economically beneficial.
° Incentives, rewards, and recognition for implementation of TQM.

° New product design that should bring together, early in the process, all who will ultimately be concerned with the product's success.
° A system in which all know their place and how they contribute to customer satisfaction.

IMPLEMENTATION

° Learn from mistakes and problems; don't try to fix blame. (Ask "Why?" not "Who?") Assessment of blame for quality failures is counterproductive; root causes must be found and corrected. (Juran's work has shown that in most instances the root causes of problems are inherent in the systems established by management that cannot ordinarily be fixed by front-line employees.)
° No constraint on improvement should be accepted as sacrosanct. If necessary, think in terms of a "clean sheet of paper." Remove constraints that create unnecessary variation, thereby reducing delay and unneeded output.
° Avoid tradeoffs by removing constraints. (For example, one can aim at *both* higher quality *and* lower costs, or reduced budgets *and* increased services.)
° Emphasis on long-term cooperative, not adversarial, relations between suppliers and customers, internal or external.
° When unions are present, emphasis on management-union cooperation rather than adversarial relations.
° Benchmarking to find best current practices, inside or outside the organization.
° Improvement can be a systematic process, often entailing "projects" aimed at specific problems or opportunities for improvement. A project proceeds in a well-defined, step-by-step sequence of activities. Often projects are implemented by cross-functional, cross-level teams or by operator teams (e.g., QC circles) within departments, but sometimes dedicated individuals can do the job.
° Rapid diffusion of best current practice; cloning and spin-off.
° Information systems that contribute to all the above, but no record keeping for the sake of record keeping.

TQM as a Strategy for Individual and Organizational Learning

Sometimes it appears that TQM simply rediscovers old truths, but it can also discover new truths. For example, recent applications of TQM methods to teaching—especially frequent fast-feedback questionnaires after individual classes (see Section 11 of Chapter 4)—have suggested ways of improving university teaching. Some of these routes to improvement are probably to be found somewhere in the voluminous research literature on educational methods. Unfortunately, finding what is relevant in the research literature may be as hard as finding the needle in the haystack, and it may not be easy to translate general research findings to the needs of a particular teaching assignment—say, to an intensive one-day course on TQM methods.

The TQM approach of improving specific individual processes can be thought of as a supplementary, or perhaps complementary, approach to searching for ideas for improvement in the potentially relevant research literature. Successful research aims at finding general principles. However, faced with a specific challenge for quality improvements, you may not find it easy to find the relevant principles nor to apply any principles you do find.

TQM, by contrast, leads to quick, specific improvements of the particular things one is doing. We may hope that general principles will emerge from combination and synthesis of what is learned from individual TQM improvement projects. But one can achieve improvements before the general principles become clear, or even when individual circumstances vary so greatly that simple general principles may not be found.

For example, the experience in trying to apply TQM to teaching suggests that a critical key to successful teaching is knowing each particular audience. Audiences vary greatly. What works well for one can fail for another. The TQM fast-feedback techniques are a good way to assess audiences. One can even size up a new audience by asking simple questions at the start of the session, with responses reported by showing of hands.

TQM as a Means to Confront Problems of Diversity

"Diversity" is a term currently used to describe the increasing heterogeneity of the U.S. workforce. Problems of diversity center on various kinds of discriminatory behavior that arise within such a workforce, with special emphasis on discrimination against females or minorities.

The first contribution of TQM to these problems stems from its posture towards improving processes rather than fixing blame. It is clear that much of the problem of discrimination is in our social processes; blaming individuals—calling them racists, for example—will not locate and remove system flaws.

At one time or another, *all* of us are victims of discrimination or at least of systematic discourtesy. Here are examples that have nothing to do with traditional race or sex discrimination:

- Residents of a nursing home, who are often assumed to be completely out of touch with reality.
- Patients in hospitals, who are often assumed to have nothing to contribute to their own diagnosis and treatment, beyond answering direct questions.
- First-year students in a service academy.
- A political/economic conservative in a liberal social gathering.
- An agnostic among a group of evangelical Christians.
- A government employee taking a holiday when other people have to work.
- Someone whose English is insecure and who finds that people tend to mumble on at full speed when distinct, slow speech would have been understood.
- Smokers almost everywhere nowadays.
- Non-degreed engineers at an engineering meeting.
- Practitioners of unconventional medicine at a medical meeting.

In all these examples, it may be of some help to the recipients of discrimination to realize that there is nothing *personal* in the bad treatment they get.

It is useful to sketch some possible types of root causes that lie behind discriminatory behavior:

1. Deep-set attitudes, mostly not based directly on experience: e.g., Serbs and Croats.
2. Attitudes based on simple statistical correlations: e.g., the car salesmen who paid no attention to a female shopper because he assumed that she was not a serious customer. (The customer went to another dealership, where she was well treated, and bought the car there.)

3. Lack of awareness: e.g., some older males who are unaware that many women do not like to be called "girls."

TQM ideas may also be useful in thinking about possible remedies corresponding to each of these classes of root causes.

1. a. Ethical/religious training: "Judge not that ye be not judged."
   b. Behavioral therapy through discussion, assuming that getting to know people better makes you like them better.
   c. Personal vision and mission statements may help.
2. Training in intuitive statistical analysis—take more variables into account, get more information; don't just judge on the basis of simple correlations. For example, asking simple questions of the female car shopper would have yielded the information that she was very serious about buying a car and was quite able to write and sign a check for purchase of one.
3. Training in giving and receiving feedback, including the use of personal quality checklists. For example, an older man could add a checklist standard not to use "girls" inappropriately.

3. HOW TOTAL QUALITY MANAGEMENT (TQM) DIFFERS FROM TRADITIONAL MANAGEMENT THINKING AND PRACTICE

For many, the ideas and precepts of TQM seem intuitively appealing, so much so that managers sometimes assume that they have been applying them all along and business school professors assume that they have been teaching them all along. These assumptions rarely stand up under close examination, which usually reveals that *some* precepts have been followed or taught but that many others have been violated. (We do not believe that TQM ideas and precepts are always correct or always applicable; that is a separate issue for research. We do believe that TQM differs in important ways from what people have always done, thought, and taught.)

Our belief that TQM is different can be best appreciated by close observation of outstanding organizations—in Japan, the United States, and elsewhere—that have successfully implemented their own approaches to TQM. The contrast between these companies and ordinary companies cannot easily be conveyed in words. Photographs of TQM factories versus traditional factories help a little: TQM factories tend to be clean, roomy, and uncluttered with in-process inventories.

We can, however, set forth TQM precepts that collide with traditional principles of management that have been, and often still are, widely taught in business schools and accepted in business practice. To show the extent of the differences, we have assembled 38 instances below. The list could no doubt be extended.

38 Points of Divergence Between TQM and Traditional Management Thinking

° Under many circumstances, choosing suppliers by competitive bidding based on lowest price has been discredited.

° It is no longer assumed that higher quality is attainable only at higher cost. When higher quality is attained by reduction of waste (or elimination of constraints), lower cost is a consequence of higher quality.

° Quality improvement and assurance are not tasks for professional specialists alone; they concern everyone in an organization.

° Final inspection as a means of achieving quality has been deemphasized, though not eliminated; the shift is to prevention of defects upstream in the process. (Improvement of quality by weeding out defects on final inspection *does* increase cost.)

° The ideas of "acceptable quality level" (AQL) and "average outgoing quality limit" (AOQL) can impede good business practice because they discourage continual improvement of quality. (Generally, any attempt to set minimum standards—however advanced they may initially seem—discourages improvement once the minimum standards have been met.)

° Really high levels of quality cannot be achieved by sampling inspection, regardless of cost.

° Management must influence or control upstream causes in *processes* in order to influence quality, costs, or profits, which are only the downstream results of processes.

° TQM has led to major changes in ideas about cost accounting. (An influential book by H. Thomas Johnson and Robert Kaplan is called, *Relevance Lost: The Rise and Fall of Management Accounting;* a useful sequel by Johnson is called *Relevance Regained: From Top-Down Control to Bottom-Up Empowerment.*)

- The feasible span of managerial control can greatly exceed the rules of thumb that have been offered in management textbooks; indeed, the term "leaderless team" has been given operational meaning.
- Tradeoffs are not inevitable. If you think that the only choice is between alternatives A and B, you may find with a little thought, brainstorming, and investigation that another alternative, say Y, dominates A and B.
- One fundamental difference between TQM and traditional management is that the latter has stressed optimization within given constraints, while TQM gives high priority to removal or relaxation of constraints.
- In aggregate, simple statistical tools, used widely, offer more potential for improvement than do sophisticated tools used only by a few specialists. (Both simple and sophisticated tools, of course, are potentially valuable.)
- Education and training conducted without opportunity for immediate application depreciates very rapidly. "Just-In-Time" training is often the goal for quality improvement projects.
- Increasing employment may be a bad response to a request to expand output; better use of current employees through process improvement should be the first thought.
- Decreasing employment is often a bad response to a request to reduce costs; better use of current employees through process improvement should be the first thought.
- It is sometimes easier to make big improvements than small ones.
- Some findings of behavioral scientists—for example, that problem-solving teams have important advantages over individuals—have relevance to business.
- Reduction of cycle time for all processes is a high-priority goal not only because speed is intrinsically desirable—say, from the standpoint of inventory costs and marketing capabilities—but because there are usually desirable side effects—for example, improved quality.
- Inventories are at best necessary evils, and constant pressure to reduce them is called for. Zero inventories are the target. Reducing inventories often reveals opportunities for process improvement.
- Employees should *not* be urged to appear busy if they have no value-adding work to do.
- Fast prototyping is a valuable strategy for new product and process development, both for manufacturing and services.

- Creativity in working around problems and backup for emergencies can *impede* long-term improvement. Good expeditors are not necessarily good managers.
- If it's not broken, it's a good time to think about developing a better preventive maintenance program.
- It is possible to bring about radical changes in organizational culture, as is illustrated by Japanese-style suggestion programs in which employees average one or more improvement suggestions *per week,* with most suggestions promptly implemented.
- It is not necessarily desirable, and may even be counterproductive, to aim for high machine utilization. However, high employee utilization is desirable, though not at the cost of producing unneeded output.
- Aside from considerations of seasonal demand by customers, producing more than the market can quickly absorb leads to serious waste.
- In many circumstances, aiming at long production runs and large batch sizes is not a wise strategy. It may be better to acquire the ability to change production setups quickly so that several product variations can be produced every day or week, thus more closely matching production and market demand.
- Persuading customers to buy something they don't really want can be a counterproductive approach to marketing. The product or service should be improved to supply what customers do in fact want.
- Special promotions, discounts, deals, and sales contests are dubious marketing tools.
- Automation and computerization are no guarantee of improved quality or lower costs; they are justified only when they can reduce variation or cut cycle time economically.
- Exhortation to do better or to try harder seldom leads to substantial and sustained improvement; specific changes in work practices and processes must be made.
- Tools and techniques for quality improvement—including use of statistics, teams, and small groups—are useful only if the organizational culture is sound, including especially the orientation towards pleasing customers.
- Middle managers and staff specialists need to emphasize training, coaching, and facilitation rather than simply giving or passing on orders.
- Traditional ideas about systems of merit ratings, incentives, and

compensation of employees have come under critical scrutiny, and the case for them has become more and more uneasy.

- Good managers must understand the specific processes of an organization; the idea that management skills are readily transferable to any kind of organization is misleading.
- In managing processes, it is essential to understand the nature of statistical variation and to try to isolate the root causes of variation.
- It is important to avoid tampering with processes that are in a state of statistical control but to search for assignable causes when the processes go out of control.
- The TQM approach is to improve reliability during product development, rather than to predict field reliability.

In commenting on this listing of differences between TQM and traditional management thinking, Willard Zangwill suggested a broader perspective: TQM entails a fundamental shift from managing through hierarchy and budgets to managing through monitoring of processes. The focus on process leads to three empirical observations:

- Waste is much more widespread than was formerly believed.
- Near-zero defects and near-zero cycle times are achievable for many processes.
- Sustained improvement, sometimes very rapid, can be achieved.

These three observations, in turn, lead to many of the propositions and observations in the list of 38 points of divergence.

TQM is not, however, universally accepted or welcomed. Certain elements of skepticism that have emerged in recent years:

- TQM sounds like a fad; TQM advocates make unrealistic claims.
- The use of an acronym like TQM for an intellectual concept is distasteful.
- In many attempts at implementation of TQM, complete frustration and disappointment, or at most limited success, is the initial result. Many employees do not buy in. (Often these attempts are based on a shallow or narrow understanding of TQM, but even well-executed attempts encounter obstacles and frustrations.)
- TQM seems to be a collection of disparate elements, not a unified body of knowledge.

° There is, as yet, little solid academic research relating to TQM.
° There does not seem to be convincing evidence that TQM works, and some quality leaders have encountered financial problems.
° There are reservations about the Malcolm Baldrige National Quality Award as a measurement of organizational excellence, especially on its alleged emphasis on processes rather than results.
° TQM puts too much emphasis on management of processes and leads to neglect of bottom-line results.
° TQM is "management by stress," just another management ploy to increase productivity.
° TQM promises long-run improvements but cannot aid in crisis situations, say when radical downsizing is needed or bankruptcy looms.

Some (not all) of these points have an element of truth, but the overall thrust, in our judgment, is wrong. It is true that TQM can be treated as a fad or program of the year. Implementation of TQM is easy to bungle. Even successful implementation of TQM for ongoing processes is no guarantee of wisdom in all areas of management, such as acquisitions.

Against this, the positive experiences with TQM implementation by the American transplants of leading Japanese companies like Honda and Toyota are persuasive. What we find here is a total change in thinking, not a new collection of tools.

The difficulties of TQM implementation deserve further consideration.

4. ISSUES IN IMPLEMENTATION OF TQM

TQM is not a distilled body of knowledge; it is a loose collection of ideas from many sources that have been successfully applied by leading companies in recent years. This body of knowledge is evolving; it is continuously improving.

When organizations try to implement TQM, there are some stunning successes, but these, unfortunately, are not the whole story. The results are often disappointing. Disappointing results, when they occur, may reflect weaknesses of the TQM ideas themselves. However, implementation is often attempted without a full grasp of the nature of TQM. Casual observation suggests that certain mistakes are made repeatedly.

Some of these mistakes could, in part, be prevented by a better understanding of personal quality. Here are examples:

° Because TQM aims at long-term improvement, even transformation, of the organization, there may be too little emphasis on obtaining initial successes, even modest successes.

Personal quality helps to correct this problem because most people who attempt personal quality checklists get at least some improvement almost immediately.

° Some TQM efforts aim at improvement of internal processes without any idea as to whether these improvements will lead to increased satisfaction of customers, internal or external.

We have stressed that standards for Personal Quality Checklists should be developed by getting suggestions from both external and internal customers.

° TQM training is often carried out long before most employees will have a chance to participate in team improvement projects, so the training leaks away and the enthusiasm is lost.

Personal quality improvement projects can and should start immediately.

° TQM training may leave out the possibility of benchmarking, of discovering and imitating better business processes.

Benchmarking can be easily illustrated and used, if on a limited scale, for personal improvement.

° TQM implementations often fail to provide motivation for employees to participate, since the benefits are not immediately apparent.

Quick benefits are often obtained from personal quality, and these make plausible the claim that similar benefits can be obtained for the whole organization.

° TQM is sometimes perceived as one more set of duties on top of everything else, and employees wonder how they will find time to do them.

The feeling of being overworked, overwhelmed, oppressed, trapped by one's job is surprisingly pervasive. Personal quality often frees up time that can be used for TQM activities for the whole organization.

- TQM programs often emphasize quality improvement teams for cross-functional problems to the neglect of individual efforts at local improvements.

  Personal quality shows that, while teams are important, individual efforts can also contribute. TQM should affect all work, not just selected improvement projects.

- TQM programs often fail to convince employees of the value of data, of the "check" stage of Plan-Do-Check-Act.

  Personal quality brings home quickly how data can be helpful and what kinds of data to seek.

- Many TQM programs fail to bring home Bob Galvin's message that quality improvement is a personal responsibility at all levels of an organization.

  Personal responsibility is the foundation of personal quality.

- Sometimes it is hard even to contemplate the possibility that removal or modification of existing constraints is possible. Substantial change in traditional ways of doing things seems unthinkable.

  Personal quality can make headway in coping even with lifelong bad work habits.

- It is often felt that "our organization is completely different, what works elsewhere won't work here."

  When you find that *you* are not completely different, you can begin to contemplate the possibility that *your organization* isn't completely different, either.

- Individual managers may be afraid of failure and hence resist trying to improve, even when the feasibility of improvement has been demonstrated elsewhere.

  Individual success reduces fear of failure at the organizational level.

- It is sometimes assumed that only small improvements are achievable by TQM.

  Both small and large improvements are achievable in personal quality. The importance of large improvements is so great that we discuss it further in Section 6.

5. HOW PERSONAL QUALITY CAN HELP

This section is an extension of the first part of Section 7 in Chapter 1.

A common element of all the difficulties in implementation of TQM in organizations is the failure to understand that TQM is more than a slogan, a program, a collection of tools, or a series of recipes. Rather, TQM is aimed at a fundamental transformation of an organization. The idea of "transformation" is hard to grasp, because the ultimately transformed organization is hard to visualize. The closest we can usually come is in terms of outstanding factories, like the NUMMI plant (Toyota/GM joint venture) in Fremont, California or the Honda plant in Marysville, Ohio. When we tour these plants, we can only marvel; if we are familiar with plants of earlier times or even many plants today, we can marvel even more. But it is very hard to relate factories to our own organizations. Moreover, on a plant tour we can see hardware, managers, and workers, but we can only sense the underlying human attitudes of the organization.

Personal quality, however, gives us a head start in understanding what organizational transformation means because we can make a modest start in transforming ourselves. In the attempted transformation, we can usually attain initial successes that, if not earthshaking, are very meaningful to us personally. The downside of every such success is the realization of how bad we were before the success was achieved. The upside is that we realize that we can look forward to further successes, not just for the next few months or years but for the rest of our working lives. Continuous improvement is just that; it never ends. Personal quality makes it easier to participate in an organization that has the same commitment to continuous improvement. Improvements do not reflect negatively on those who originally developed the process that was improved. And instead of being surprised by each improvement, we come to *expect and plan for further improvements.*

Moreover, personal quality weakens the resistance to change. We *can* contemplate the possibility of removal or modification of *any* constraint. We can fight the tendency to reject anything that was Not Invented Here. We can more easily remember that, as Zangwill has put it, good ideas are born dumb: that is, the first version of a new idea may not be very useful, but it can be developed and refined into something that is very useful.

Personal quality can help to instill the customer orientation that is almost totally absent in so many organizations, yet absolutely essential to Total Quality Management. The standards on personal quality checklists should always be defined with customers—immediate or ultimate—in mind.

Embracing of personal quality by senior management drives home to them the point that the organization's drive cannot fully succeed without their active participation. Cheerleading may help morale a little, but it is an inadequate substitute for leading by personal example.

Self-Assessment

Following a suggestion of the late Perry Gluckman, an insightful quality consultant, we propose that everyone in an organization make a self-assessment, by asking the question: "What things about my job bother, annoy, or frustrate me most?"

The first task is to make a list of perhaps five or ten aspects. Then consider the question: "Which aspects can I change, improve, modify, or constructively work on without having to obtain approval from anyone else? That is, which aspects are *controllable* by me?" These aspects may suggest standards for your personal checklist.

The uncontrollable aspects on the annoyance listing have at least two major components:

1. Bad company policies and practices; poor organizational culture.
2. Individual frictions with co-workers, superiors, and subordinates.

Personal quality can make a start on a weak point of organizational culture, as in the improvement of meetings at AT&T. Individual frictions are a different problem. The perfection that is sometimes attainable in manufacturing is probably beyond reach in interpersonal relations. But for the frictions that exist within natural work groups, we can see an important contribution of personal quality. Members of the work group can ask each other for helpful standards for their Personal Quality

Checklists, just as Sergesketter asked his associates for suggestions on his revised checklist. See also Section 8 of Chapter 1, "Group Use of Personal Quality Checklists."

6. SCHAFFER'S BREAKTHROUGH STRATEGY, AND ITS IMPLICATIONS FOR PERSONAL QUALITY

"Continuous improvement" is a fundamental tenet of TQM. But as Bob Galvin says, it is also desirable to have *dis*continuous improvement, that is, breakthroughs or home runs. Galvin's company, Motorola, has set and substantially met very ambitious targets, targets that require breakthroughs as well as continuous improvement. For example, Motorola sets goals on improvement, to be met in all parts of the company: cut error rates by two thirds *each year*, and cut cycle times by 50 percent *each year*. General Electric has an approach called "Workout" that is aimed at fast improvements, "quick hits." Such goals are more than mere slogans of the kind Deming deprecates; they are achieved by drastic reduction and even removal of constraints *within a relatively short time* once it is seen that the constraints stand in the way of the goal.

Both authors feel that they have scored home runs—or at least extra base hits—with their personal quality checklists. We have received similar testimonials from many others. Although our emphasis is personal quality, we feel that a development of the ideas of major improvements at the organizational level will have substantial carryover to personal improvement. Hence the balance of this section will be devoted to a discussion of organizational breakthrough and its implications for personal breakthrough.

Robert H. Schaffer has written a book called *The Breakthrough Strategy* (New York: Ballinger, 1988) that probes into this remarkable phenomenon. The following discussion follows Schaffer's arguments closely.

When strongly challenged by a crisis, some organizations can improve quality and productivity *enormously*. An example is Exxon's Bayway Refinery in Linden, New Jersey:

- Workforce had been reduced from 3000 to 2700 to become "lean and mean."
- Strike ensued (anticipated to be of short duration).

- 450 supervisors, managers, and engineers decided to try to keep the refinery operating for a short while.
- "This makeshift team had to postpone major maintenance projects, of course, but they ran the refinery well. They ran it safely. They delivered product 'on spec' and on time. And they did it not just for a few days, but for four months."
- " . . . The people who ran it, instead of feeling resentment at being overworked, actually seemed to feel a special sense of drama and excitement, which they had never experienced in the organization before. It was an adventure, a challenge, and they talked about their feat for years after."

Memories of a successful challenge are cherished by participants. But when the challenge is past, there is typically a reversion to the previous lower level. This occurs because of built-in barriers and constraints, both organizational and psychological. These same barriers and constraints tend to doom ambitious organization-wide "programs," TQM or otherwise: "Perpetual Preparations Waste Billions" because organizations feel they can't improve anything until they improve everything.

Another example is the Bonaventure Express Terminal of the Canadian National Railway.

- Steadily deteriorating service quality.
- A string of consulting firms studied terminal layout; handling of materials; scheduling work flow; no improvement.
- A team of company industrial engineers tried work sampling, crew scheduling and supervision, productivity and performance measurements; no improvement.
- A human-resources approach followed: train supervisors; survey employee attitudes and try to improve them; involve employees in problem solving; conflict resolution; no improvement.
- Performance kept deteriorating.
- Finally, they focused on one key train, No. 242, from Toronto to Montreal, which had been loading only 45 to 50 percent of the shipments earmarked for overnight delivery. Goal: increase the percentage to 80 percent in the *next few months*, without affecting service on any other trains.
- They reached the goal in a *few weeks*.

Learn from crises; why do they stimulate radically higher perfor-mance? Schaffer identifies a number of zest factors:

- ◦ "Sense of urgency"
- ◦ "A challenge"
- ◦ "Success near and clear"
- ◦ "People collaborate—a new esprit"
- ◦ "Pride of achievement"
- ◦ "Fear of failure"
- ◦ "Exciting, novel, like a game"
- ◦ "People experiment and ignore red tape"

This leads to the *project approach,* aimed at a "tangible, bottom-line *re-sult* in *a short period of time,*" and "carried out in ways that generate the new management confidence and new management skills necessary for fur-ther progress."

Schaffer's breakthrough approach is related to Juran's approach to TQM: "All improvement is made project by project and in no other way." (Note that Juran's projects are not necessarily interdepartmental team projects; they may be individual projects or intradepartmental team projects. Also, Juran's projects are aimed at small improvements as well as major breakthroughs.)

Implications for Personal Breakthrough

Breakthroughs are possible also at the level of personal quality. Some-times the Personal Quality Checklist alone is a sufficient stimulus for breakthrough. When it is not, you can supplement your personal check-lists with special personal breakthrough projects.

One approach to personal breakthrough is suggested by Schaffer. You may find it helpful to think back to see if there have not been times in your life in which you have been forced by emergencies to undertake projects that resulted in major personal breakthroughs. What were the circumstances? How did you do it? Did you learn any lesson that you can apply now? Answers to these questions may provide clues to per-sonal breakthroughs in the future.

Another approach to breakthrough ideas is your experience with the checklist. As you keep improving on your individual standards, you also get insights into other aspects of your work habits or personal performance that are not touched directly by the checklist standards. Sometimes these can serve as a basis for additional standards and a revised checklist. Sometimes, however, they can provide the basis for personal breakthrough projects that go beyond the personal checklist methodology.

In either approach, you select a goal that you very much want to meet, trim it down if it's too ambitious, and *set a relatively short time limit for its achievement.* The short time limit prevents you from unrealistic fantasizing about what you can do. For example, one friend has recently gained a lot of weight and says that he will not run another 10K race until he loses twenty pounds. A better approach would be to say that he will run a 10K race as soon as he loses three pounds, and then to register for a race that is, say, six weeks in the future.

Remember that the key to breakthrough is not necessarily working harder, going without sleep, trying consciously to do something spectacular: rather, it is finding and removing constraints that are inhibiting your current performance. You must do something different from what you have always been doing.

CONCLUSION

George MacDonald, in a spiritual context, said, "There is endless room for rebellion against ourselves." (C.S. Lewis, ed., *George MacDonald, An Anthology*, [New York: Macmillan, 1947, p. 45]). We as individuals all have the potential for never-ending quality improvement, both incremental and breakthrough, in the way we do our work and lead our lives. The principles of quality are as applicable to services as to manufacturing. They are as applicable to individuals as to organizations, and individuals can put them into effect more rapidly than can organizations. Moreover, although we often complain of poor quality in our organizations, our personal quality may be equally in need of improvement.

We know that some of the best company suggestion systems elicit an average of *more than one implemented improvement per week per employee*. Why can't individuals make one *personal* improvement—however modest—per week? Why can't individuals carry out personal quality improvement projects in the same way as teams carry out improvement projects within organizations? Why can't individuals use statistical ideas to improve their own health or to find more time to do things they have always wanted to do but couldn't?

This brings us back to where we started, to Bob Galvin's statement, "You must be a believer that quality is a very personal responsibility." We are all responsible for our own work and can dramatically impact the quality of that work. It does require setting standards based on customer requirements, measuring defects and cycle time against those standards, and, in general, drawing on quality principles for never-ending improvement.

We hope you will begin your Personal Quality Checklist now if you have not already started. Keep it simple and learn as you go. Bring in additional quality tools as you progress; some of these may serve you well even if you don't care for the checklist approach. Improving your personal quality will make you more valuable to your customers, your associates, your family, your friends, and yourself. We are on this planet Earth such a relatively short time. Let's make the most of it.

APPENDIX

ELEMENTARY STATISTICS TUTORIAL BASED ON PERSONAL QUALITY

1. STATISTICS IN TOTAL QUALITY MANAGEMENT

Many people think of statistics as both dull and difficult. Statistics courses, unfortunately, have contributed to that image. In this chapter, we shall try to give a more positive view of statistics by bringing out a few very important ideas in the context of an application of the Personal Quality Checklist by a sales vice president who deals with customers in the steel industry.

We shall use his daily data for the first seven weeks. The key information is shown in the computer printout shown below. The quality standards are represented by the names listed across the top; brief explanations are printed out following the data. Each row of numbers represents the number of defects for one of the 49 days of his study.

#LIS-TEN	DOO-DLE	IM-PATNT	DELE-GATE	PRO-FANE	PROMPTPH	PROMPTQU	FIT-NESS	SWEETS	TOTAL
0	0	0	0	5	0	0	1	6	12
1	2	0	0	7	0	0	1	10	21
2	1	3	1	13	0	0	1	2	23
0	1	0	0	10	1	0	1	1	14
0	0	4	0	8	0	1	1	1	15
3	0	2	0	12	0	0	1	2	20
0	0	0	0	3	0	0	1	1	5
1	1	0	0	7	2	1	1	2	15
0	1	2	0	9	0	1	1	2	16
0	0	2	0	5	1	1	1	3	13
2	0	0	0	5	1	1	1	1	11
3	0	1	0	9	1	1	1	0	16

#LIS-TEN	DOO-DLE	IM-PATNT	DELE-GATE	PRO-FANE	PROMPTPH	PROMPTQU	FIT-NESS	SWEETS	TOTAL
0	0	1	0	3	0	0	0	1	5
0	0	0	0	3	0	0	0	2	5
0	1	0	1	3	0	0	1	0	6
0	0	0	0	6	0	1	1	1	9
1	1	1	0	3	0	0	1	0	7
0	0	0	0	4	1	0	0	0	5
0	1	0	0	6	1	1	1	0	10
0	0	0	0	2	0	0	1	3	6
0	0	0	0	2	0	0	0	1	3
1	0	0	0	1	0	0	1	0	3
0	0	0	0	0	1	0	1	1	3
0	0	0	0	6	0	0	1	0	7
2	0	1	0	5	0	0	1	4	13
3	1	0	0	8	1	0	1	0	14
0	0	1	0	2	0	0	1	0	4
0	0	1	0	1	0	0	1	0	3
1	0	0	0	5	0	1	1	1	9
0	0	1	1	5	0	1	1	1	10
2	0	0	0	4	0	1	1	2	10
1	0	0	0	3	0	0	1	0	5
0	0	0	0	2	0	1	1	0	4
0	0	2	0	4	0	0	1	0	7
0	0	0	0	3	0	0	1	2	6
0	0	1	1	5	0	1	1	0	9
0	0	0	1	6	0	0	1	0	8
0	0	1	0	3	0	0	1	0	5
0	0	1	0	3	0	0	1	4	9
2	1	0	0	2	0	0	1	4	10
0	0	0	0	1	0	0	1	4	6
0	0	0	0	2	0	0	1	0	3
0	0	0	0	0	1	0	1	0	2
1	0	0	0	3	0	0	1	0	5
0	0	1	0	2	0	0	1	5	9
0	0	0	0	3	0	0	1	0	4
0	1	0	0	2	0	0	1	5	9
1	0	1	0	3	0	0	1	2	8
0	0	0	0	3	0	0	1	3	7

```
#LISTEN:    realize I have missed an important
#           point in a discussion because I let
#           my mind wander.
#DOODLE:    doodling during business phone
#           conversations.
#IMPATNT:   letting impatience show in voice or
#           body language.
#DELEGATE:  failure to delegate.
#PROFANE:   use of profanity (each profane word
#           is one defect).
#PROMPTPH:  prompt return of phone calls.
#PROMPTQU:  complete request for a sales quote
#           in one day.
#FITNESS:   exercise 5 times a week; weight
#           under 195 pounds.
#SWEETS:    limit candy intake to two pieces
#           per day.
```

Three of these standards are primarily personal: PROFANE, FIT-NESS, and SWEETS. You may be interested in his rationale for PRO-FANE and SWEETS:

PROFANE: "In general, steel mill personnel express themselves by using "*&$#" at nearly every other word. The nine-plus years that I have been associated with the steel mills have impaired my language skills because I have substituted this 'colorful language' into most of my sentences. On more than a few occasions, I have tried to reduce my swearing, but without much success."

SWEETS: "The humongous sweet tooth buried in my head doesn't allow me to eat a couple pieces of candy; it is not satiated until everything is consumed."

2. PRELIMINARY PARETO ANALYSIS

After the first week of use of the checklist, information became available to give some idea as to which of the standards were going to be most difficult to cope with and where the greatest opportunities for improvement lay. His 110 defects were divided among the nine standards as follows:

Standard	Frequency	Cumulative Frequency	Percent	Cumulative Percent
PROFANE	58	58	52.7%	52.7%
SWEETS	23	81	20.9	73.6
IMPATNT	9	90	8.2	81.8
FITNESS	7	97	6.4	88.2
LISTEN	6	103	5.5	93.6
DOODLE	4	107	3.6	97.2
PROMPTQU	1	108	0.9	98.2
PROMPTPH	1	109	0.9	99.1
DELEGATE	1	110	0.9	100.0
Total	110		100.0%	

It is seen that two of the nine standards—PROFANE and SWEETS—account for nearly three quarters of all defects. If defects under all standards are equally serious, these two categories would be singled out for most intensive, highest priority efforts at improvement.

This simple analysis to determine priorities has been called "Pareto analysis" by Joseph Juran. Wilfredo Pareto was an Italian economist who studied inequality in the distribution of wealth. Actually it was Juran himself who pointed out that for categorical data in a wide range of applications, a small fraction of the categories usually contributes a large fraction of the total occurrences. For instance:

- A small fraction of the defect categories contributes a large fraction of the defects, as in the example above.
- A small fraction of a company's products contributes a large fraction of the company's sales (unit sales or dollar sales).
- A small fraction of a company's customers contributes a large fraction of the company's sales.
- A small fraction of the causes of accidents accounts for most of the total accidents.
- A small fraction of students in a class contributes a large fraction of the questions that are asked.
- A small fraction of possible explanatory variables accounts for most of the explanation in statistical regression studies.
- A small fraction of a company's quality problems accounts for a large fraction of the company's costs incurred because of bad quality.

In our application Juran would term PROFANE and SWEETS the "vital few" and the remaining categories the "trivial many" (more recently, he says the "useful many"). If remedial efforts are undertaken, the priority is given to the vital few. Thus the vital few quality problems in a company should receive the major and earliest attention in the company's TQM efforts. The useful many problems can be tackled later, perhaps by individuals or small work groups such as Quality Circles.

In the present personal example, the simple frequency count of defects may not be a fully accurate guide. A defect under PROFANE, for example, may not be as serious as a defect under PROMPTQU— prompt sales quote. To deal with this problem, the frequencies under each standard might be given a relative weight, weighted frequencies might be computed, and Pareto analysis applied to the weighted frequencies. For example, if a defect under the strictly business categories is counted at face value, it might be decided that 10 defects on PRO-FANE would be counted as one weighted defect—so that there would be 5.8 adjusted defects for profanity.

3. RUN CHART FOR TOTAL DEFECTS

How did the checklist work overall in the first seven weeks? A simple graphical answer is shown in the run chart in Figure 6, in which total daily defects are plotted vertically versus days or "time" horizontally.

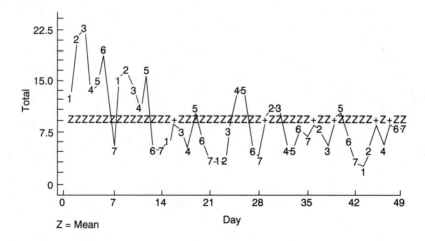

Figure 6

("Run chart" is a term used by quality professionals; statisticians usually call it a "time series chart," "time sequence plot," or simply "time plot.")

The numerals 1, 2, 3, 4, 5, 6, 7, 1, 2, . . . are used to denote the points. This tells us at a glance which day of the week is involved; for example, all 1s are Mondays, all 4s are Thursdays.

Successive points are connected by line segments in order better to bring out the sequential behavior of the data in Figure 6.

Qualitatively, this picture is similar to that shown for Sergesketter in Chapter 1: steep decline at first, then a flattening out. It doesn't take formal statistical analysis to show that "significant" improvement has occurred: informal visual analysis tells the story. In fact, here we have another illustration of Berkson's Interocular Traumatic Test (ITT): the message of the data does in fact hit us between the eyes. Recall that the aim of TQM should always be big improvements, even though all improvements, small as well as large, are welcome.

The mean number of total defects per day was 8.8. The horizontal line traced out by the Zs on the run chart is at height 8.8. This helps the eye better to trace out the down trend shown in the data: in the early part of the period, most points are above the line; later most points are below.

If you are paying close attention, you will notice that the 7s—Sundays—tend to be consistently low, as is shown in Figure 7, where the 7s are shown in boldface.

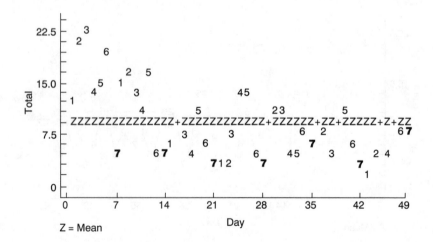

Z = Mean

Figure 7

This Sunday effect is an example of what is called a "periodic" or "seasonal effect." For full understanding of what is going on in the data, we want to be able to detect seasonal effects. In this instance, the ITT can do the job.

4. STATISTICAL FITTING OF SYSTEMATIC EFFECTS

The visual analysis, ITT, has revealed two systematic effects in the data:

1. A downtrend, rapid at first and slower later. With Personal Quality Checklists, we are always hoping for a downtrend.
2. A day-of-the-week, or seasonal, effect: fewer defects tend to occur on Sunday than on other days. This has nothing to do with the aimed-for quality improvement, but it is valuable information.

You could simply sketch a freehand curve on the run chart to describe your impressions about these two systematic effects: that is, you could sketch a curve for the downtrend and modify it for a lower value on Sundays. Figure 8 shows such a curve derived from statistical computation, the *values fitted by statistical regression*, which are traced out by the Zs:

It is interesting to note here that the fitted values actually start turn-

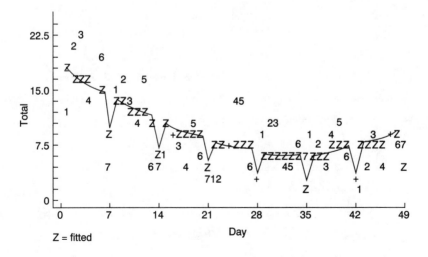

Z = fitted

Figure 8

ing *upward* in the final few days, suggesting that some backsliding is occurring. There is an obvious need to hold the gains, or at least to prevent further backsliding. We shall later come back to this issue.

This chart is central to the role of statistics in quality improvement. Whatever process and whatever measure, when we intervene in the hopes of improving the process, we hope to have evidence of a significant improvement in the basic trend, which is estimated by the fitted values. Recall the example of improving the putting process from Chapter 4; Figure 9 shows the corresponding run chart with statistical fitted values:

In this application, the fitted values for percentage of successful putts before the change of stance formed a horizontal line at height about 56. After the change of stance, the fitted values jumped to a horizontal line at height about 64. Thus, there was evidence of a sudden improvement.

In the checklist application, the run chart pointed to a gradual improvement: the fitted values for defects tended downward, rapidly at first and then more slowly, and finally turned upward. Overall, there was substantial improvement, but there was also a hint of backsliding at the end.

In both these examples, the ITT alone gives clear indication of the improvement achieved. Sometimes, however, visual evidence alone will

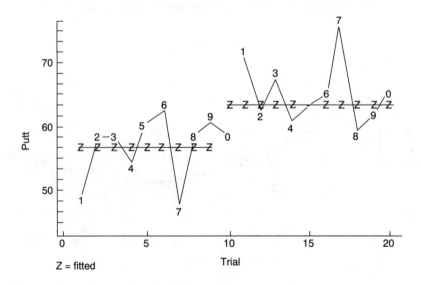

Figure 9

not suffice to indicate clearly whether or not improvement occurred. Then we need the formal statistical calculations to clarify whether or not success has been achieved. *Whenever we attempt quality improvement, we must check our success by display of the run chart for the basic process measure that we are trying to improve.* And the visual analysis of that run chart is always the first step, whether or not the formal statistical computations are carried out later. So, whether or not you know about the technical statistics, the moral is: *Look at the run chart to help decide whether you have succeeded.*

5. A MORE DETAILED EXAMINATION OF THE CHECKLIST RESULTS

So far we have looked only at the run chart of total defects per day. The corresponding run charts for some of the individual standards will provide additional insight. All can be satisfactorily analyzed by the ITT.

First, consider the two most problematic standards suggested by the Pareto analysis after the first week's results, PROFANE and SWEETS. Again, the Sundays are in boldface; not surprisingly, profanity was lowest on Sunday!

The downtrend, rapid at first and then slower, which was seen on Figure 8, for TOTAL, is clear here, except that there is little hint of an upturn at the end. The Sunday effect is also clear. The run chart for SWEETS (Figure 11) tells a somewhat different story:

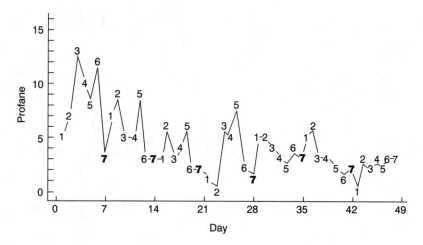

Figure 10

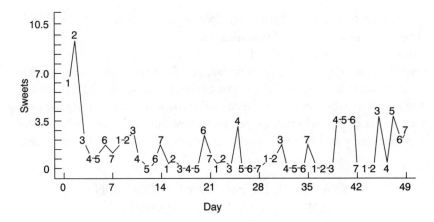

Figure 11

Now we see some improvement in the first two or three weeks, but then the evidence of backsliding near the end is substantial. Here may be the key to the problem seen at the end of run chart for TOTAL.

Another important aspect is the total defects per day on the six purely "business" standards: LISTEN, DOODLE, IMPATNT, DELEGATE, PROMPTPH, and PROMPTQU. Figure 12 shows the run chart for that total, named BSDEFECT.

Here progress seems to have been maintained through the entire seven weeks.

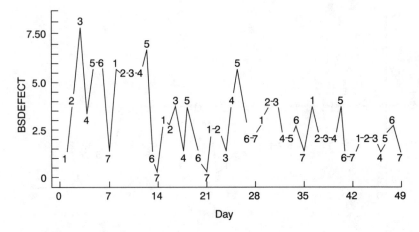

Figure 12

Finally, we report briefly on the remaining "personal" standard, FIT-NESS. Here there were only four defect-free days in the entire 49 days. Apparently no progress was made. However, defects were defined either by missing a workout or recording a weight in excess of 195 pounds. It may have been that he was not missing workouts but was almost always heavier than 195 pounds. (We know that he is a very serious runner.) It might have been well to separate out the two components of this standard.

In general, however, we have found that people who choose FIT-NESS for a standard have a tough time in improving, although there have been a few conspicuous successes.

6. RUN CHARTS AND CONTROL CHARTS

A prominent statistical tool for monitoring a process is called a control chart. It is essentially a run chart with upper and lower "control limits" drawn in to show the limits between ordinary and unusual observations. Unusual observations, sometimes called "outliers," can reflect *special causes* or *sporadic causes* that should be sought out when a point on the control chart falls outside the control limits.

The control chart is primarily a tool for "holding the gains." It is assumed that *the process is in a state of statistical control*, which means:

1. The data tend to vary about a constant level through time.
2. The deviations from the constant level have about the same variability through time.
3. The most recent deviations are of no help in predicting the direction (above or below the constant level) for the next deviation.
4. In common applications, it is assumed that the data follow a normal distribution.

If a process is in a state of statistical control, the chance of a point lying outside control limits is only about 3 in 1000. Therefore, when a point is found outside the control limits, there is a suggestion that a special cause has occurred. If so, we want to investigate to find and correct the special cause. This is one good way to "hold the gains."

The data in the putting example appeared to be in control before the intervention, and then in control at a higher level after the intervention.

The checklist data were *not* in statistical control: visual analysis, confirmed by statistical fitting, clearly revealed trend and day-of-week ef-fects. *If the process is not in control, it is incorrect and misleading to go through the formal statistical computations to obtain control limits and to plot these limits on a run chart.* Figure 13 shows what happens if this advice is ignored:

UCL stands for "upper control limit" and LCL stands for "lower con-trol limit." (These are calculated by a computer program using a stan-dard formula that need not concern us here.) We see that three early points are above the upper control limit. Does that mean that we should search for special causes?

We know that the answer is "No." We have seen that there is a strong trend effect that operates through the seven-week period. The level of defects started high and then sharply dropped, due to the checklist ef-fect. The three early points above the upper control limit occur at the early stage of use of the checklist: they do not reflect a special cause; rather they fit well into the overall picture.

We can profitably look at another control chart arising from the same data. The deviations of actual daily defects from the fitted values dis-played in Section 5 are called *residuals:* These tell how far each point is above or below the fitted value. Residuals are indicated in Figure 14 by the vertical segments on the original run chart for TOTAL:

These residuals *are* in a state of statistical control, as you can see from the control chart in Figure 15.

No residuals are outside control limits, and visual analysis of this con-trol chart (Figure 15) suggests the 3 items listed on page 145.

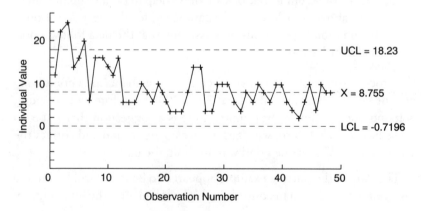

Figure 13 Control Chart for TOTAL

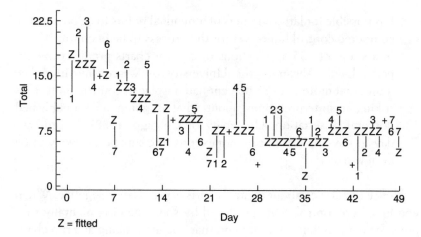

Figure 14

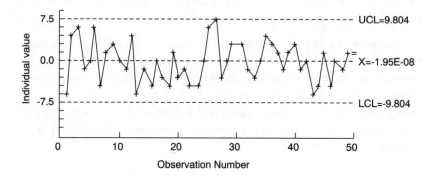

Figure 15

1. The residuals tend to vary about a constant level (zero) through time.
2. The residuals have about the same variability through time.
3. The most recent residuals are of no help in predicting the direction (above or below the constant level) for the next residual.

For processes of interest in TQM, it is relatively unusual to find a state of statistical control. Even when you have obviously improved the process substantially, you may not have succeeded in putting it into a state of statistical control. In the absence of statistical control, computed control limits are potentially seriously misleading. For example:

° It is possible for all the points to be within the computed control limits, yet for the process to be badly out of control.

° It is possible for large numbers of individual points to be outside the computed control limits, yet for the process to be in control.
° In a study of 235 applications of control charts produced by experts, Layth Alwan of the University of Wisconsin/Milwaukee found that more than 85 percent had misplaced control limits, thus risking misinterpretations about what is going on (unpublished doctoral dissertation, University of Chicago, 1988). In ordinary day-to-day applications by nonexperts, the situation is likely to be even worse.

Hence our advice about control charts is necessarily negative. When you look at a control chart produced by someone else, mentally suppress the control limits and pretend that you are looking at a run chart. Then apply the ITT—simple visual analysis—to the run chart. Look for trends, "seasonal" patterns, or other departures from the three guidelines given above for a process to be in a state of statistical control.

Of course, if you learn more about statistics, you can become a more discerning user of run charts and you will know when to use control charts. You can learn to do statistical fitting, and you can apply formal statistical checks that go beyond the ITT. But our exhortation to do careful visual analysis of run charts will help you to learn what can be learned from the data, and avoid common misinterpretations from inappropriate control charts.

Statistical Control Is Not the Only Objective

If a process is in a state of statistical control, as described above, it is essentially "stable." TQM aims at stable processes. But stability is not the only desirable objective. We want stability at a high performance level. Thus we want defects to be in control at a low level, and we want to continue to reduce that low level. Similarly, we want golf scores to be in control at a low level, and we want to continue to reduce that low level.

You Don't Have to Wait Until a Process Is in Control
Before You Start to Improve It

In the putting example, the process was in control before the change of putting stance. The change of stance led to a process improvement; afterwards the process was in control at a higher level of successful putts.

Sometimes it is believed that we must put a process in control by removing special causes before we can start systematic attempts to improve it, such as the change of stance in the putting application. The personal quality defect data above show that this is false. The defect level was never in control, but it was substantially improved during the seven-week period.

If a process is in control to begin with, it may indeed be easier to detect process improvement (by the ITT or by formal statistical analysis) because the uncontrolled process variation has a simpler pattern, a pattern sometimes called "random." But even if there are trends, seasonal patterns, and other systematic sources of variation—as in the defect data—we can try to make allowance for the effects of these effects by statistical analysis. Thus if, after the seventh week, our sales vice president had decided to deal with the SWEETS problem by trying to substitute diet candy for regular candy, we could have seen whether the subsequent defects dropped from what would have been expected from the previous trend and seasonal effects.

Statistical Control, Control Limits, and Tampering

If a process is in a state of statistical control, there will of course be variation through time, but the *individual* variations convey no useful information about how to improve the process. Nonetheless, people are tempted to make improvements based on these individual variations. Suppose, for example, that your golf scores through time are in statistical control but that you finish a round with a relatively high score. Your first thought is that something must be wrong and that you must do something about it: change your stance, grip, or stroke; buy a new set of clubs; take lessons; and so on.

Making such ad hoc changes when a process is in control has been called "tampering" by Deming. There is both theoretical reasoning and practical experience to suggest that tampering makes processes worse. Here is an extreme example. During World War II, Roberts had an opportunity to zero in his M1 rifle (that is, set the sights correctly) by unlimited use of a rifle range for a whole afternoon. (The weather was ideal, and there was no wind.) He reasoned that he would fire from the prone position (which is very steady), check the deviation of the resulting shot from the bullseye, and adjust the sights to compensate for the error. He thought that one or two shots would suffice to get the right setting of the sights.

After a whole afternoon of firing, he found to his chagrin that he was no closer to being zeroed in than he had been at the start. Deming uses a "funnel experiment" to explain why this type of tampering is bad. It turns out that the sight changes were *increasing* the dispersion of impacts from the bullseye, and that the precise amount of increase can be predicted on the basis of statistical theory.

What Roberts should have done was to fire, say, ten or twenty rounds without touching the sights, make a statistical analysis of the *average* horizontal and vertical deviations from the bullseye, and adjust the sights accordingly.

Had he known about control charts, he would have been protected from his folly even if he hadn't understood Deming's funnel experiment. He could have computed control limits on his horizontal and vertical deviations. So long as all points were within the upper and lower control limits, he would have known that ad hoc adjustments were counterproductive and that he should not tamper with the sights.

7. APPLICATION: BORDERLINE HYPERTENSION

The next item deals with quantitatively measured data to illustrate some simple statistical tools. For several years, Roberts has had occasional blood pressure readings in the range called "borderline hypertension"—often defined by a systolic pressure of over 140 or a diastolic pressure of over 90. Recently, when being treated for a minor infection, he was measured at 160/94, which caused some concern to the physician. Subsequently, Roberts decided to monitor his own blood pressure using an electronic blood pressure meter. He wanted both to see how he was doing and to see whether exercise seemed to have any immediate effect on blood pressure.

The data below refer to the month prior to the writing of this section. The readings were all made in the late evening of the day. "NEWO" (for "no evening workout" is 1 when there was no earlier evening workout, and 0 when there was. When there was an earlier workout, the type of workout is indicated by "HH" for light weights, "JOG" for jogging, and "WT" for indoor cycling on a racing bicycle mounted on a wind trainer. In each case, the days on which such workouts occurred are indicated by 1, while 0 denotes their absence.

#SYS	DIAS	PULSE	NEWO	HH	JOG	WT
144	93	45	1	0	0	0
145	88	48	1	0	0	0
143	79	50	1	0	0	0
139	89	43	1	0	0	0
120	86	53	0	0	0	1
130	83	55	0	0	0	1
128	73	40	0	1	0	0
146	82	48	0	0	0	1
134	83	49	0	1	0	0
148	81	47	0	1	0	0
144	89	50	1	0	0	0
150	89	47	1	0	0	0
142	82	47	1	0	0	0
142	78	51	0	1	0	0
127	86	55	0	0	0	1
138	79	48	0	0	1	0
157	90	51	1	0	0	0
132	80	53	0	0	0	1
148	86	50	0	0	1	0
144	93	50	1	0	0	0
155	92	52	1	0	0	0
143	94	51	1	0	0	0
144	83	47	1	0	0	0
155	92	45	1	0	0	0
139	82	44	0	0	0	1
149	86	50	0	0	1	0
135	83	55	0	0	0	1

#Late evening blood pressure readings and
pulses, September 18—October 16,
#1992, Harry Roberts. (September 29, 30
missing due to travel.)
#SYS: systolic reading
#DIAS: diastolic reading
#PULSE: pulse rate
#NEWO: no workout within preceding two hours
#HH: half-hour workout with light weights
within preceding two hours
#JOB: 1 1/2 miles jogging within preceding two
hours

```
#WT: 24 minutes indoor cycling (wind trainer)
#On all days there was at least one daytime
workout
```

When the variable NEWO was equal to zero, there was no workout in the evening before the blood pressure measurement.

The systolic and diastolic readings are plotted in time order on the run chart in Figure 16.

The Interocular Traumatic Test here suggests two main conclusions:

1. Many of the systolic readings are above the borderline of 140, and some diastolic readings are above the borderline of 90. (The mean of all systolic readings was 141.5, and the diastolic mean was 85.2.)
2. It appears that the systolic readings are trending upwards.

We can pursue the analysis by investigating the effect of evening workouts. First, we look at the systolic readings and show in boldface the evenings in which a workout was missed (Figure 17).

With this additional plot, which shows the bold number to be gener-

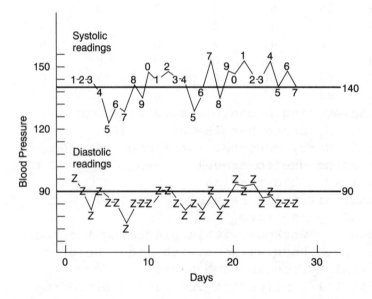

Figure 16

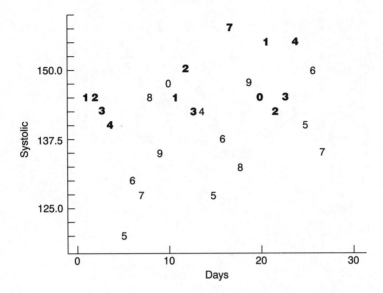

Figure 17

ally high, the interocular traumatic test suggests that the systolic pressure tended to be higher on days when evening workouts were missed. Hence, in addition to the uptrend previously noted, we seem to have identified a second systematic effect: exercise. The trend effect is bad, while the exercise effect is encouraging.

Both effects can be investigated formally by the statistical tool of *regression analysis*, mentioned in Section 1. This analysis gives us a prediction formula—"regression equation"—for systolic pressure, which is shown below:

Predicted SYS = 131 + 10.2 NEWO + 0.392 TIME

This is read as follows: Predicted pressure equals a constant 131 plus 10.2 points for missed workout plus a trend value that increases 0.392 units per day (or about 4 units every 10 days). Both systematic effects— exercise and trend—are "statistically significant," which means roughly that we can't write them off as chance flukes of this sample of 27 days. The interocular traumatic test has served us well!

The regression can be visualized as in Figure 18, where the Zs trace out the predicted or fitted values given by the above regression equation.

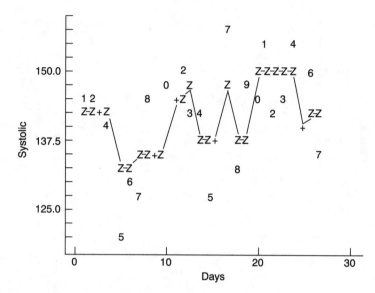

Figure 18

You will see two clumps of Zs: The top clump (no workout) is trending upwards in the 140s, while the bottom clump (workout) is trending up in the 130s.

Now we look at the diastolic readings (Figure 19).

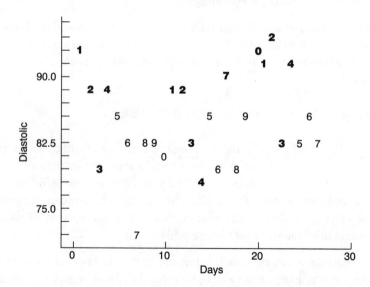

Figure 19

The exercise effect is again pretty clear on visual examination, so we try out regression again:

Predicted DIAS = 80.0 + 6.88 NEWO + 0.140 TIME

Thus predicted pressure is 80 plus about 7 points for a missed workout plus a time trend that goes up about 1.4 points every ten days. The exercise effect is statistically significant, but the trend effect is not significant by the usual standards of statistical significance. Also, the trend, if real, is more gradual than for the systolic readings.

Again, we can visualize the analysis by a single plot in Figure 20.

There are two important conclusions:

1. The trend effect—especially for systolic—is a warning that the problem may be getting worse. Trends call our attention to something that is causing steady change, but they don't identify the causes. One possible cause lies in the fact that the early observations occurred during the last part of the academic interim period, while the later observations occurred during the start of the autumn term, when increased stress occurs. Whatever the cause, it is clear that continued monitoring is in order.

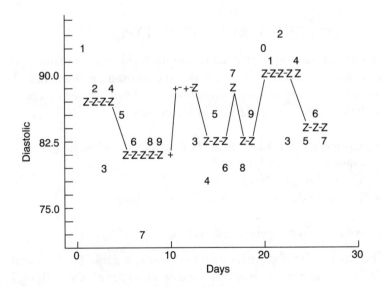

Figure 20

2. The exercise effect suggests one means of dealing with the problem: A workout seems to lower blood pressure. Further investigation would be needed to see how long the effect lasts and whether some forms of exercise are more effective than others. Additional work with the above data set suggests that the stationary biking on the wind trainer is more effective than the jogging (which was much less vigorous than Roberts's usual daytime running workouts) or the light weights.

We have not mentioned one important qualification to the analysis. Roberts tended to miss workouts when he felt that he needed to do more work on a particular evening (say, working on this book). It is possible that the fact that he was working late on the evenings when he did not exercise may have caused stress that tended to increase blood pressure. Hence stress rather than, or in addition to, exercise may have been a causal variable. Against this possibility is the fact that he did at least some work on most of the evenings when he later worked out.

Statistical analysis cannot by itself resolve this ambiguity about causation. From a statistical point of view, a better way to have experimented with the effects of exercising would have been to have used some form of randomization to decide which evenings would include workouts and which would not. (In the next section, we will explain and illustrate this possibility.)

8. APPLICATION: A POOL EXPERIMENT

A student had been using an unconventional technique for playing pool: unorthodox upside-down V bridge and eye focused on object ball. The standard technique called for closed bridge and eye focused on cue ball. Thus there are four combinations of technique:

1. Upside-down bridge, object ball (student's technique)
2. Upside-down bridge, cue ball
3. Closed bridge, object ball
4. Closed bridge, cue ball (standard technique)

Which of these four combinations is best?

The student defined performance on a single game by the variable SHOTS, the number of shots from the break to get all the balls in. He did his study in blocks of four consecutive games, a different technique combination for each game. The order of the four techniques was chosen randomly. The idea of random ordering is this: write the numbers 1, 2, 3, 4 on four cards. Shuffle the cards thoroughly and write down the shuffled order, say 3, 2, 1, 4. Try the techniques in that order.

Then repeat for each block of four consecutive games.

The ideas behind random ordering is to avoid the shadow over causal interpretation that was mentioned in the blood pressure example. Due to the randomization, the order of using the techniques will tend to be unrelated to other variables, such as fatigue or practice effects, that might affect the student's scores.

On each day he played two blocks of four consecutive games, so he played eight games per day. He did this for five days, so he played 40 games in all. Here is the data set and details of the design.

```
#MORROW.ASC
```

#SHOTS	SESS	BRIDGE	EYE
50	1	1	-1
39	1	1	1
43	1	-1	-1
78	1	-1	1
62	1	1	-1
40	1	-1	-1
62	1	-1	1
62	1	1	1
32	2	1	1
36	2	-1	1
48	2	-1	-1
45	2	1	-1
54	2	-1	1
46	2	1	-1
55	2	1	1
50	2	-1	-1
39	3	1	1
58	3	1	-1
44	3	-1	-1
56	3	-1	1
62	3	1	-1
57	3	-1	1

46	3	1	1
52	3	-1	-1
40	4	1	-1
41	4	-1	1
27	4	1	1
46	4	-1	-1
48	4	-1	1
32	4	1	1
52	4	1	-1
50	4	-1	-1
35	5	-1	-1
38	5	-1	1
33	5	1	-1
25	5	1	1
40	5	1	-1
52	5	-1	-1
45	5	-1	1
36	5	1	1

```
#Study to improve game of pool
#SHOTS:  the number of shots from the break to
         get all the balls in
#BRIDGE  = -1 for unorthodox upside-down V
         bridge (starting method)
#        = 1 for standard closed bridge
         (standard method)
#EYE     = -1 eye focused on object ball
         (starting method)
#        = 1 eye focused on cue ball
         (standard method)
#SESS:   session, eight games per session on a
         given day, five sessions
```

We display SHOTS on the run chart in Figure 21, where the games in each day are numbered 1, 2, 3, 4, 5, 6, 7, and 8, so that you can see which day was which:

The interocular traumatic test suggests that he was trending downwards, towards improvement (lower scores), throughout the experiment.

Next, look at the data by days; remember that there are five days with eight games each (Figure 22).

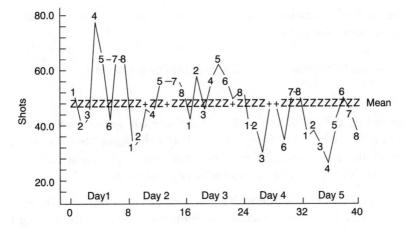

Figure 21

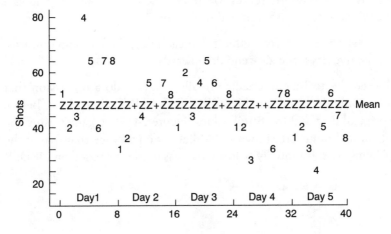

Figure 22

Now you will have to sharpen your eyeballing of the data, but if you look carefully at the above data day by day, you will see a *tendency* for the points to rise within each day. There is apparently a fatigue effect operating within the eight games played on each day.

It is important to emphasize that this process was *not* in a state of statistical control. Systematic factors—trends—were causing the out-of-control condition.

Regression analysis permits us to sort out the effects of the nonrandom factors *and* the technique variations.

In the final regression by ordinary least squares, the sources of variation are sorted out as follows.

Predicted SHOTS = 48.0 − 9.96 STANDARD − 0.459 TIME + 2.29 ORDER

Translation: the predicted number of shots equals a constant 48 minus 9.96 for the standard technique minus 0.459 shots per game for trend over all 40 games plus 2.29 shots per game within the eight games of each day. All the variables are statistically significant.

The practical conclusion is that the student's unorthodox technique was harmful. He should swallow his pride and change to the standard technique.

To visualize how the regression tracks the data, Figure 23 shows a plot analogous to the ones shown in Section 7.

It is easy to see the trend effects. For each day, the Zs trend upwards. Over the five days, the Zs trend downwards.

To see the technique effects visually, we first do a regression that involves only the trend variables ORDER and TIME, then plot as before the original data and the fitted values (Figure 24). The games using the standard technique are shown in boldface. You will see that five of the bold items are substantially below what was predicted based on ORDER

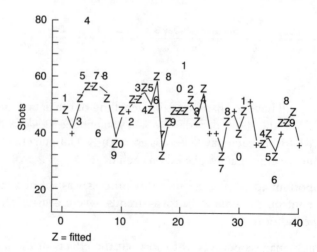

Figure 23

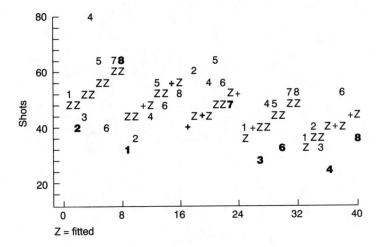

Figure 24

and TIME; two were about the same; and one was slightly above. This suggests that the standard technique tends to give lower (better) scores by comparison with what would have been expected from the trend effects.

INDEX

ABOUT THE AUTHORS

Harry V. Roberts is the Sigmund E. Edelstone Professor of Statistics and Quality Management in the Graduate School of Business at the University of Chicago. He is the author or coauthor of more than 10 books and 60 articles on subjects related to statistics and Total Quality Management.

Bernard F. Sergesketter is Vice President, Central Region, for AT&T. He is a recipient of the Outstanding Electrical Engineer and the Distinguished Engineering Alumnus Awards from Purdue University, and he is the first recipient of the AT&T Quality Award for Sales Excellence.